ESSENTIAL GUIDE OF

WHISKY

David Dalmau, editor

editors

© EDITORS, S.A. 2018

C/. Horts d'en Mateu, s/n.
Pol. Industrial Sur
08450 Llinars del Vallès
Barcelona ESPAÑA

ISBN: 978-84-459-0954-6

Author: Editorial Team, VVAA
Translation: Ile Heinrich

ESSENTIAL GUIDE OF

WHISKY

editors

INDEX

ONCE UPON A TIME THE SCOTCH...

With a genius that no other people have been able to overcome, the Scots have turned a simple cereal liquor one of the most diversified spirits in aroma and strength. Taking advantage of each of the scarce resources of a poor and inhospitable country, they have managed to combine pure water, barley, peat and sea air to invent the widest range of whiskies in the world.

With insistence, the Scots say that the quality of their whiskies comes first of all from the purity of the water in their springs. It is true: in the absence of large urban concentrations, intense agriculture, and heavy industries, the essential characteristic of Scotland and particularly the Highlands, is that is an area ecologically well protected from pollution. In addition, its water is weakly mineralized (especially in lime), which prevents the formation of unpleasant tastes during the manufacture of whiskies.

But the claim of this quality is also a way of proclaiming that only in Scotland you can get a good whisky, and nowhere else, because of this geographical dependence on water. This statement is only relative (there are excellent whiskies that are not from Scotland), and further evidence contradicts it: in some regions, such as Speyside or even the island of Islay, neighboring distilleries, use the same water and the same raw materials, producing very different malts.

The Scottish whisky resides mainly in four columns that are based on a know-how, developed over the centuries: peat, distil, aging in barrels and mixtures.

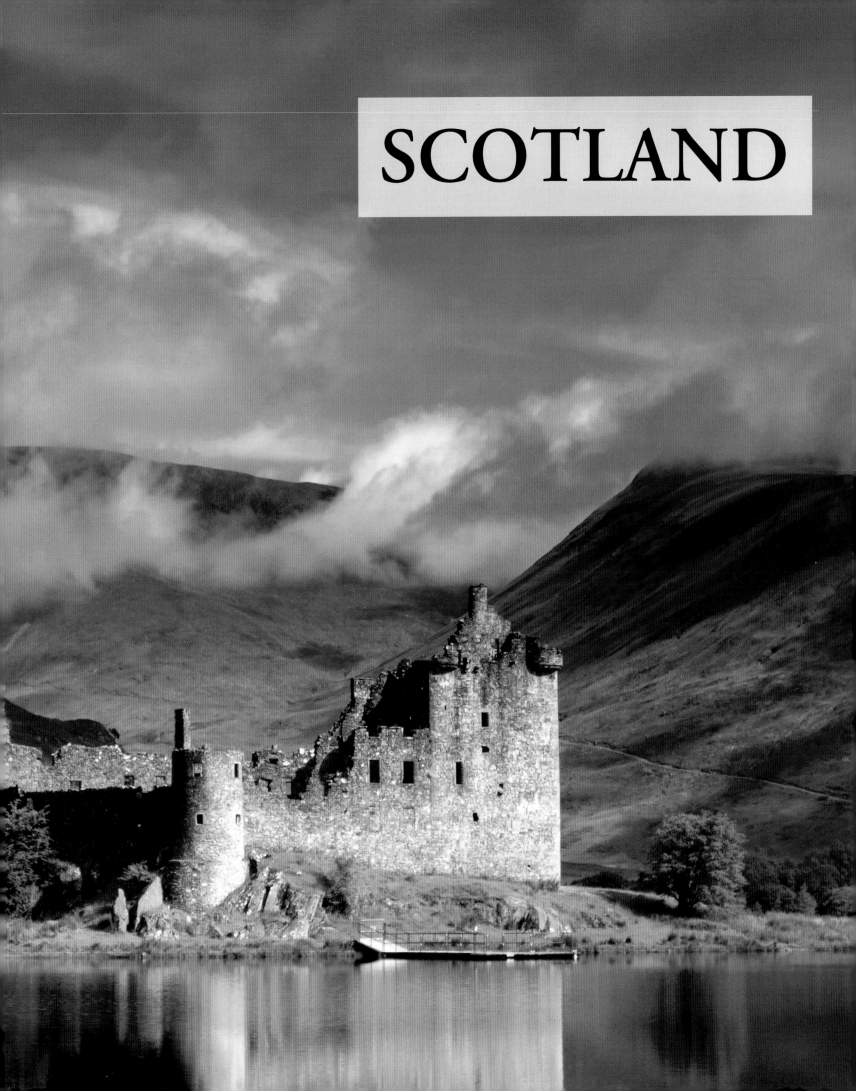

SCOTLAND

THE MAGIC OF THE PEAT

Take the case of the peat. This mediocre fuel comes from the marshes formed in the Quaternary era, at the time of the decomposition of vegetables. Containing only 60% carbon (against almost 100% in the best carbons), it burns badly and gives off a lot of smoke and strong smells. But the Scots have taken great advantages from these drawbacks. Settling near the peat bogs, the first distillers took advantage, in fact, of this abundant and easily extracted fuel (a shovel is enough), and also of the water of the nearby marshes, where it is loaded with specific aromas, transmitted to the liquor during its manufacture and its bottling. For the transformation of barley into malt they also used peat. This was ideal: its slow combustion is very appropriate for the drying operation of the barley, that requires some time. And its odorous fumes transmitted to cereals some specific aromas that were and are one of the qualities of Scotch whisky.

The very nature of the peat played its part. In the islands, for example, it contains more 'varechs' in decomposition, which provides some interesting marine and iodine notes. In addition, it was more marked because of briars. Over the centuries, the Scots have learned to dose the amount of peat needed to differentiate the whiskies. Some do not even use it (especially in the lowlands), others, like in the islands, consume it in bulk. This produces a particularly varied aromatic range.

THE ALCHEMY OF STILL

The secret of a good spirit is its distillation. Without going back to improbable Chinese or Arab distillers, that nobody has demonstrated that they practiced twice distillation, indispensable, the technique is the same as that of many centuries ago. And the process of distillation is still not very clear, at least on the theoretical level. Its knowledge and mastery are above all the result of know-how and renewed experiments that constantly give new information. Since the multiple compounds that are processed and transformed in the still under the action of heat have not yet been really identified, and especially their influence on the aromatic and gustatory plane is still widely unknown. In the absence of a satisfactory theoretical model, true knowledge is drawn from practice. And history has allowed the Scots to be the true Einstein of the matter.

As soon as it was known (perhaps by the Irish), the distillation of whisky was indispensable to the Scots, since only it could pro-vide a complement of resources to farmers who lived miserably from their poor lands, and they were not even the owners of that lands. In many cases, this was the only way to pay the rents claimed by the landlords. The story of John McDonald, the famous Long John, is exemplary in this regard: son of a family ruined by his nationalist convictions, from a young age he learned to distill in the family farm, taking advantage of the legalization of distillation.

As soon as it spread through the Scottish lands, it provoked a lively reaction from the authorities. From 1644, the first taxes appeared, and throughout the eighteenth century the agents of the English tax authorities fined clandestine distillers. But how to control an entire people, who was also so proud of its national identity?

This threat played a real role in the formation of the art of distillation, providing the discovery of new techniques and obtaining unexpected results due to the hiding. When legalization finally arrived in 1823, a generation was formed that only had to transform its *know-how* into an industrial and commercial success

The secrecy especially taught to distillers the importance of the shape of the still for the final result. Depending on the size, height of the neck or upper part of the still, the length and curvature of the swan neck, the obtained liquors are more or less aromatic, more or less fine. Each distiller thus created his style. Likewise, when a distillery is accidentally destroyed, the stills are reconstructed identical to the previous ones. If, however, the distillery is new, the stills must be the same as the old ones from other distilleries.

It also remains the conduction of the distillation. At what point should the selection of «heart of the Chaldean» be made, eliminating the beginning and the end of the distillation? Each family (as in Glenfarclas or Glenfiddich) has its practice, transmitted from one generation to another, to maintain an identical result. And if the owner often changes the distiller, the *stillman* remains in place and passes on his knowledge to his successors.

THE AGING TIME

Another well-kept secret is that of aging. This is more recent than that of distillation. The *smugglers,* the clandestine of whisky, should not have much time to let their liquors grow old, except in a few hiding places hidden and abandoned for several years. In spite of its apparent strength, the oak barrel where the recently distilled whisky is put is not an airtight container but a real colander. The exchanges between alcohol, wood and oxygen are permanent and complex, significantly influencing the qualities of the final result.

The contribution of the Scots consisted above all in taking advantage of the facilities that they obtained with the trade of wines and liquors. The taste of the English for port and sherry, whose fashion dates back to the eighteenth century, provided them with large quantities of oak barrels that served to transport those wines to Britain. With its contact, the whisky gains new aromas and a more pleasant harmony than the hardness contributed by the barrel of new oak. Also, these oak barrels were cheaper, fact that did not bother

at all. The operation was renewed in the twentieth century, with American bourbon. In effect, the North American legislation demanded the use of new barrels, the used ones were a true treasure for the Scots, because in them the scotch ages very well and they are more economic. Thus, an authentic commercial circuit was set in motion: the Scots recover the barrels of bourbon that the Americans do not know where to put... to then sell their whiskies to the United States.

Over the years, the Scots have been combining all the aromas provided by the barrels. The proportions vary from one distillery to another. Macallan, for example, uses almost exclusively sherry barrels, to the point of made them in Spain and making in them sherry for three or four years before using them for their precious malt.

We have to do some concession to the geographical determinism, because the Scottish malts truly resent the place where they age. In Islay or in the Orkney islands, the barrels are placed a few meters from the waves and the marine winds, with which the malts gain in their unique aromas, especially iodized ones,

SCOT, SCOTTISH AND SCOTCH

In English, a Scotsman is a scot, and the equivalent adjective is Scottish. The word scotch refers almost exclusively to whisky, except for its use in some culinary expressions. In this respect, the term «scotch whisky» is almost a pleonasm for a Scotsman.

that surprise from the moment in which the bottle is opened and continue long time in the mouth after having taken a sip. There is obviously nothing of all this in the malts that have aged quietly in the depths of the Highlands. Only the mildness of the Scottish climate remains, never warm but not too cold, a decisive factor in the aging quality of whiskey, which is not subject to sudden climatic changes. In this regard, the case of Campbeltown (Springbank) is evident: the constant softness provided by the Gulf Stream lends great harmony to the malts there.

THE SECRET OF THE BLEND

Like the cava, scotch whisky would not have surpassed perhaps the level of a regional product, much appreciated but without great future, if the idea of assembly had not taken place. This technique rests on a worthy postulate of Euclid: the final result of the sum of several elements far exceeds its simple sum. In quality, obviously...

The legalization of 1823 allowed the Scottish distillers to get out of hiding, although they were not assured of wealth. They were able, in effect, to sell their products easily in the region, but once they passed the Cheviot mountains, which form the symbolic border between Scotland and England, in the absence of a geographical one, their rough and powerful malts were not very successful. In London clearly preferred gin, then sherry and bordeaux, more distinguished than spirits from barely civilized regions. Even Queen Victoria's passion for her beloved Balmoral Highlands was little interested in the level of malt sales. The situation changed little by little with the invention of Robert Stein, in 1827. This distiller of the Lowlands launched a new still, improved in 1831 by Aeneas Coofey, tax inspector. Its apparatus had the advantage of being able to distill continuously, while with classic stills, the «pot still», similar to that used in Charentes for cognac, it was necessary to empty the apparatus once the distillation was carried out, and to reload it. The new «still» can work without interruption, which is much cheaper, if only in labor. It also produces spirits of greater finesse, although they are less aromatic. In short, accept even un-malted cereals, such as wheat and, above all, corn, if you add some boiled malted barley at the beginning. Fast and economical, the «still» had all the advantages and with its invention soon industrial distilleries were created, which lacked, of course, the charm of the Highlands, but which generated great benefits, if only by providing the manufacturers of gin a purified alcohol.

When the Usher, father and son, launched a whisky that linked cereal spirits and malts

THE WHISKY REGIONS

The division of Scotland into four main regions is based on geographical reasons, but especially on the different styles of whisky. The separation between Highlands and Lowlands, according to an imaginary line that goes from Greenock to the West, to Dundee to the East, dates from the Wash Act of 1784, a fiscal law. Within the Highlands, the region of Islay Island and Campbeltown have been delimited. Speyside, in the heart of the Highlands, constitutes a specific subset.

The Lowlands, between Glasgow and Edinburgh, is first and foremost the region of cereal distilleries to make mixtures (or blends) (there is only one in the Highlands, in Invergordon). These are large, highly automated factories, installed near ports to facilitate the arrival of raw materials and the exit of whisky boxes. There are also four malt distilleries. Malts have a particular style, clear and light, and are often made by triple distillation, as in Ireland. In the Highlands are most of the distilleries of malt, almost a hundred considering those who have temporarily close. This very disparate set involves very precise areas:

-the islands of the West (Skye, Jura, Mull), where the malts marked by the sea breeze are elaborated, however without pretending to imitate the characteristic style of Islay;

-the Northern Highlands, to which the Orkney Islands are usually incorporated;

-the Speyside, in the center of the Highlands, where the largest number of distilleries is concentrated. Their malts are appreciated for their elegance and harmony. The Glenlivets are a subfamily of them, once famous for the recognized quality of The Glenlivet. But the malts, more and more, abandon this reference, authorized by a law of 1880, preferring to affirm their autonomy and their specification.

Islay, the great island of the West, has eight distilleries and defines a particular style, marked by the power, the taste of smoked and the sea breeze. But there are important variations between each malt.

Campbeltown, south of the Kintyre peninsula, is a few kilometers from Ireland («to a cormorant flight» is often said there). This proximity suggests that it was probably here that the first Scottish malts were made. A century ago there were more than thirty distilleries there, but only two remain. However, the style of Campbeltown is still considered specific, different from that of the other malts.

to the market, they were not the first to have had the idea of mixing whiskies from different origins. The «vatted malt», or « malt out of the vat», was not a novelty, and many owners of cabarets had already had the same idea. But the Usher blend was one of the first to be commercialized, in 1853.

The aromatic force melted thus with the softness and the delicacy of the cereal whiskies. And this seduced the palate of the British, and after the whole world.

The mixer soon became a strong and respected professional. He worked and works essentially with his nose, identifying each one of the contents of the vats he gathers, so that they harmonize in a specific way. Moreover, the appearance of the mixtures coincided with the birth of real brands, often identified by the name of its owner. These brands associated different whiskies, at least a dozen, and often three or four times more, coming from different regions of Scotland and of more or less important age. The objective was to obtain a product constant in quality and flavor, which was clearly identified by the consumer and, therefore, easy to sell.

Il was with the blends that in Scotland a true whisky industry was created. Its national success, and later international, allowed to create new distilleries and to favor the economic start-up of the most disinherited regions of the Highlands or the islands. Long John, Johnnie Walker, the Chivas brothers, James Buchanan, John Haig, John Dewar, Arthur Bell, William Sanderson, were some of the pioneers.

Such success did not materialize without regrets and protests. Thus, in the 1890s, the Pattison brothers launched a blend with great advertising boast, but it was of such dubious quality that their adventure ended in a resounding bankruptcy.

A few years later, it was necessary to appeal to the courts to determine if the blend deserved the name of whisky. In 1906, the court of Islington, in the municipality of London, ruled that only malts deserved such a name. But the angry mixers appealed to a real commission. After dozens and dozens of meetings, of witness hearings, of trips (including those made even to Charentes), and of multiple and comforting tastings, apparently, a generous sentence was pronounced: malts and spirits, mixed or not, were entitled to the much-desired name. In the following years, the law required a minimum aging of two years, and after that, three to deserve such a title. Later, apart from distillation and mixing, bottling was already mandatory in Scotland to obtain the official name. But it had been a long time since the scotch had conquered the world...

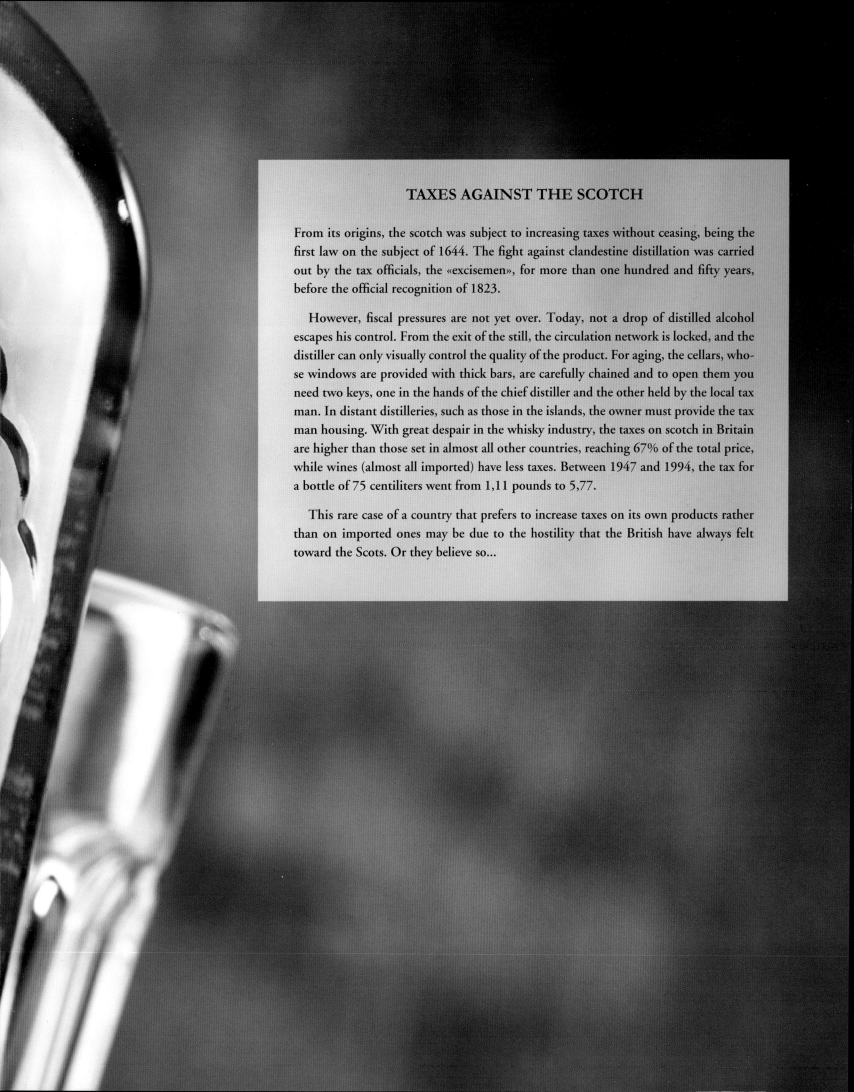

TAXES AGAINST THE SCOTCH

From its origins, the scotch was subject to increasing taxes without ceasing, being the first law on the subject of 1644. The fight against clandestine distillation was carried out by the tax officials, the «excisemen», for more than one hundred and fifty years, before the official recognition of 1823.

However, fiscal pressures are not yet over. Today, not a drop of distilled alcohol escapes his control. From the exit of the still, the circulation network is locked, and the distiller can only visually control the quality of the product. For aging, the cellars, whose windows are provided with thick bars, are carefully chained and to open them you need two keys, one in the hands of the chief distiller and the other held by the local tax man. In distant distilleries, such as those in the islands, the owner must provide the tax man housing. With great despair in the whisky industry, the taxes on scotch in Britain are higher than those set in almost all other countries, reaching 67% of the total price, while wines (almost all imported) have less taxes. Between 1947 and 1994, the tax for a bottle of 75 centiliters went from 1,11 pounds to 5,77.

This rare case of a country that prefers to increase taxes on its own products rather than on imported ones may be due to the hostility that the British have always felt toward the Scots. Or they believe so...

Aberlour

Type: **single malt.**
Origin: **Highlands (Speyside).**
Owner: **Campbell Distillers (Pernod-Ricard).**
Date of birth: **1826.**

Located not far from the confluence of the rivers Lour and Spey (from which it takes its name Aberlour, which means mouth of the Lour), the distillery was born under the best auspices, because the spring from which it gets its water is called «well of Saint Dunstan». That Christian missionary was one of the great evangelists of Scotland in the tenth century, and he chose that spring to celebrate baptisms before becoming archbishop of Canterbury in 940.

Created by James Gordon, the distillery dates from 1826, that is, barely three years after the legalization of whisky. Served by a water of great quality out of the Ben Rinnes, it flourished quickly, despite a fairly hectic existence. In 1840, its new owner, a banker named James Fleming, installed it in another site located almost a kilometer away from the first site. In 1898, a violent fire devastated it, but according to the chronicles of the time, the essentials of the whiskies were saved in the casks. Acquired in 1945 by Campbell Distilleries, Aberour becomes the property of the French group Pernod-Picard in 1974, when it buys the Scottish company. For long time, Aberlour malts have only served for the manufacture of blends, and it was only in 1972 that the first single malt bottle was commercialized. The best-selling quality is currently the ten years old (which has replaced the twelve years of the beginning), but Aberlour also exists in older versions —the Mary Stuart of fifteen years of age, the vintages of 1970 and 1971-, mainly destined to the French market and to the «duty-free» stores.

With a beautiful dark color, especially due to the use of casks that have previously contained bourbon or sherry for maturation, Aberlour whisky is distinguished by its great aromatic harmony. His qualities have allowed it to get a gold medal and the «Pot Still» trophy of the international wine and spirits contest twice (unique case), the great annual Scotch whisky contest, in 1986 and 1990.

On the occasion of this contest, the vintage of 1964 was presented. And the legend states that that year, the well of St. Dunstan, for some time almost silent, began to flow again with unusual vigor... Chance or magic? We will never know.

The Scottish Land, kingdom of rams and briars.

Auchentoshan

Type: **single malt.**
Origin: **Lowlands.**
Owner: **Morrison-Bowmore.**
Date of birth: **1800.**

Located north of Glasgow, Auchentoshan is the best representative of the distilleries of the Lowlands. Against the powerful whiskies of the Highlands, they produce much smoother, rather pale whiskies, ignored by the experts for a long time. However, its aromatic delicacy deserves to be tasted, and it ages very well: there is a twenty-one-year-old Auchentoshan very appreciated for its harmony and its scents of cedar and vanilla.

At the beginning of the 19th century, the whiskies of Auchentoshan were preferred to the North ones by British society precisely because they were less strong. But the development of the blends, from 1860, eliminated them and all the production was quickly destined to the blends. Founded around 1800, the distillery was built at the foot of the Kilpatrick Mountains, from where its water comes. It was largely rebuilt after the Second World War and modernized in 1974. Ten years later, it passed to the group Stanley Morrison (later Morrison-Bowmore), who wanted to expand the range of its whiskies, Bowmore in Islay, and Glen Garioch in the Highlands.

In the traditional style of the Lowlands, and as in Ireland, Auchentoshan whiskies go through a triple distillation in large-capacity stills, which gives them greater softness and a very high alcohol level, around 85°. It also has the advantage of giving a liquor that ages much more quickly, reaching its optimal state at seven or eight years, which satisfies the mixers. But, as it was said before, the qualities that age for a longer time are not the least interesting.

AND ALSO...

Aberfeldy
This powerful whisky, from the center of the Highlands (the distillery goes back to 1898), is used primarily for the development of Dewar's (United Distillers). It is always available in bottles of fifteen years of age.

The Antiquary

Once made by a subsidiary of Sanderson (Vat 69), that bland belongs to United Distillers today. Taking its name from a novel by Sir Walter Scott, it is distinguished above all by its bottle with cut sides, of ancient form, and at the moment it is practically unique in its kind, in Scotland.

Ardbeg
This ancient distillery of the island of Islay (dates back to at least 1794), had some time the characteristic to perform the malting of their barley. Particularly strong, this whisky did not enjoy much of the favor of the mixers, and the distillery closed in 1983, resuming its activity six years later, but without the malting. Currently only a ten-year-old whisky distilled in 1983 is available.

Ardmore
Neighbor of Speyside, the distillery of Ardmore mainly produces a whisky for the Teacher's blend. But a small part is bottled for independent distributors.

Aultmore
Located in Speyside, this distillery belongs to the United Distillers group, which mainly uses its whisky for its different blends (especially Dewar's). Today, a small amount of twelve years of age is bottled.

Balblair

Type: **single malt.**
Origin: **Northern Highlands.**
Owner: **Caledonian (Allied Distillers).**
Date of birth: **1749.**

Located in a valley between mountains, with green pastures where flocks of lambs and sheep pass, the Balblair distillery offers one of the most pastoral images of the Northern Highlands, a region much less austere than its name might suggest. There the peat bogs are important and the water of the springs contains specific aromas due to a very original flora. The small town of Edderton is called «the parish of the peat», coal that is drier and more easily pulverized there than in other areas.

Near the Carron river, that flow into the Dornoch Firth and from there goes to the sea, the place has always seduced the distillers... and the smugglers. Balblair was created in 1749 (which makes it the second oldest in Scotland, after Oban) or, according to other sources, in 1790. But most of the current facilities date back to the late nineteenth century.

Like the other malts in the region, Balblair has a spicy character, because of the aromas of the peat. But its great freshness and lack of strength means that experts have rejected it for some time. The main parts of the production have been reserved for the production of Ballantine's blends, after Balblair acquired the Hiram Walker group in 1979. For some time, only independent bottling companies (Gordon and MacPhail) have proposed ten-year-old Balblair whiskies, every time the distillery only sold five-year-old whiskies, light and clear, early matured. But the situation evolved as the group Allied Distillers created a specific subsidiary, the Caledonian Malt Whiskey Distillers Limited, to market its catalog of single malts (Laphroaig, Tormore, etc.) of which Balblair is part.

Ballantine's

Type: **blend.**
Origin: **Glasgow.**
Owner: **Allied Domecq.**
Date of birth: **1865.**

One of the best-selling Scotch whiskies worldwide is named after a man of very modest origins, George Ballantine, born in 1809, in Broughton-Home, an agricultural region near Edinburgh. Only his father, Archibald, farmer and descendant of farmers, is known of his family, although it is known that he was related to more famous Scots, such as the Bellenden and the Bannatyne, who became known as warriors, wise and administrators from the 15th century.

From the age of thirteen, the young Ballantine worked as an apprentice in an Edinburgh grocery store, owned by a guy William Hunter. Very well endowed for that office, five years later he opened his own store in the district of Cowgate, in the same city.

Scotland was experiencing a real economic boom at the time, and the business of George Ballantine benefited of it. In 1842 he married the daughter of a grain merchant and settled in a more elegant district, specializing more and more in wines and liquors. George Ballantine was, above all, a merchant and knew how to guess the evolutions and offer the products that attracted the most customers.

No doubt that this was the reason why he left Edinburgh in 1865 and left his business to his eldest son to create a new trade in Glasgow with his other son. He quickly developed the liquor trade, achieving a good clientele in England and Ireland, and even beginning to export whiskies, whose blends he himself guarded.

After giving up the business in 1891, George Ballantine has as successors his sons, then his nephews, who continued his commercial policy of quality, taking whiskies and also wines as centerpiece.

brand, which played a large role in the global liquor business. However, its leaders sensed the formidable future of Scotch whisky, particularly in North America, and wished to be the owners of a well-established brand of fame. Then, they acquired some brands, such as Courvoisier cognac, Maker's Mark bourbon and Kahlua coffee liqueur. A year after this purchase, Ballantine's was equipped with a new cereal distillery, located in Dumbarton, north of Glasgow, one of the largest in Europe, while acquiring other malt distilleries.

Also, after the Second World War, Ballantine's had all the advantages to be one of the first international brands, thanks to a well-adapted marketing.

THE INTERNALTIONAL DIMENSION

While continuing to grow, the business of George Ballantine was, after the First World War, without successors who wanted to deal with the company, until two men, Barclay and McKinlay, resumed the activities.

Paradoxically, the birth of the Ballantine's brand is due to them, since previously neither George Ballantine nor his successors had ever used the family name as a brand, despite their reputation, and often sold their whiskies with the original name, like Talisker or The Old Glenlivet.

Barclay and McKinlay also continued

the development of the society, putting the accent almost exclusively on the whisky, as well as acquiring new distilleries and wineries in all Scotland. They devoted themselves especially to the export, in particular to the United States, where they counted among their travelers with one David Niven, later famous theater and cinema actor.

But the economic obstacles, such as the era of prohibition, and the financial crash of 1929, reduced their monetary possibilities and they decided it was prudent to resell the company to the Hiram Walker group in 1937. This Canadian company, founded in the mid-nineteenth century, had made fortune with its Canadian Club

In 1987, Ballantine's passed to the British group Allied Lyons, which already had great brands (Teacher's, Long John, etc.), but it was in Dumbarton where they installed the headquarters.

As the last avatar of the internationalization of the liquor business, Allied Lyons merged in 1994 with the Pedro Domecq group, number one in sherry and cognac.

ATTENTION TO QUALITY

In a specific bottle, slightly rectangular, Ballantine's Finest is a rather light blend, but of an interesting complexity, and is characterized by its great aromatic harmony, with a tiny peat spot.

It is true that the group has the means to guarantee a perfect continuation in the quality of its blends. It has, in fact, fourteen malt distilleries, spread over the Orkney islands and the island of Islay, as well as the best regions of the Highlands, including Speyside.

Two distilleries (Dumbarton and Strathclyde) provide the cereal whisky, and the aging cellars are spread out in different parts, some of which (Willowyard and Dumbuck), have been guarded since 1959... by white geese, baptized as the «guards of the scotch» (scotch *watch*). They feed on the grass that surrounds the cellars, and those birds are known for their squeals and aggressiveness, thus monitor almost 270 million liters of whisky. Protection that is judged effective, because since their arrival has not been detected even a single robbery. And the goose has become the official logo of the brand.

Ballantine's also owns its own malting shop, Robert Kilgour, in Kirkcaldy, whose inspectors monitor the quality of the production of the barley harvests that will be used to make the malts. Manufactured from at least forty different malts, Ballantine's Finest represents more than 90% of the brand's sales, with the rest divided among three other varieties: Gold Seal twelve years; Ballantine's seventeen years; Ballantine's thirty years, much harder to find. Very exported, Ballantine's is the number one brand of scotch whisky in Europe and third in the whole world.

Some goslings, future guardians of Ballantine's stores.

The Balvenie

Type: **single and pure malt.**
Origin: **Highlands (Speyside).**
Owner: **William Grant & Sons.**
Date of birth: **1892.**

Located in Dufftown, the «capital» of Speyside whisky, Balvenie is a castle that stands on the hill overlooking the town. At the beginning of the thirteenth century, the third Earl of Buchan decided to build it, and later became the property of the Scottish crown. However, King James II later gave it back to his owners, with two conditions: that Lady Douglas marry Sir John Stewart, one of his faithful lieutenants, and the lady gave him each year, in vassalage, a red rose. This is why there is still a rose on the blazon that is reproduced on the Balvenie label. The castle, in the 17th century, became the property of Alexander Duff de Braco, who gave his surname to the neighboring town.

A similar past had to inspire William Grant when he acquired in 1892 the buildings next to the first distillery, Glenfiddich, created five years earlier. Giving him the name «The Balvenie», he installed a second complete distillery, with its own malting, a large supply of barley from the fields of the domain, and eight stills with necks much longer than those of the neighboring dis-

tillery. The cunning of William Grant and his successors was to produce a malt very different from that of Glenfiddich. However, the water is identical, but the science of the distiller revealed itself in the elaboration of a much more aromatic and more powerful liquor, with honey tones, particularly original.

The malting, very far from Glanfiddich's, is of higher rank, as well as aging. Indeed, the Balvenie ages, in part, in new casks, but also in others of fine sherry, or with a strong scent. This produces a sumptuous malt, very appreciated for good digestion. Founder's Reserve, for a long time the only reference available from The Balvenie, is a ten-year-old malt, whose bottle has for long time simulated the shape of a malting oven door. With increasing success, other varieties are now possible: the Double Wood, a twelve-year-old whisky, whose maturation started in a new oak casks (for strength), and continues in a sherry cask (for its roundness); the fifteen-year-old Single Barrel, coming from a single barrel and sold in numbered bottles.

Bell's

Type: **blend.**
Origin: **Perth.**
Owner: **United Distillers.**
Date of birth: **1865.**

At the origin of the business is a wine and liquor store in Perth, founded in 1825 by Thomas Sandeman, a member of the famous merchant family in Porto. The latter hired in 1845 a young representative, Arthur Bell, who experienced an ascent that can be described as very rapid, and six years later he was associated with the owner, until taking the reins of the company in 1865, finally giving him his first name.

Arthur Bell was one of the first to believe in the development of blends. «Several fine whiskies mixed, he wrote, please the palate of many people, more than a single unmixed whisky. It's been a while since I

Very mountainous, the region of Fort William always close to the sea.

adopted this practice and the qualities of my products speak for themselves».

Aided by his two sons, Arthur Kinmond and Robert, Arthur Bell proved to be a formidable salesman. He was the first Scot to open an office in London, in 1863, and tried since then to normalize the sizes of liquor bottles. Since the end of the 19th century, the Arthur Bell blends were widely exported, not only to Europe, but also to Australia, New Zealand and the Indies. But it was not until 1904, four years after the death of its founder, that his name became the brand of the main whisky sold by society. Its expansion continued during the interwar period, with the conquest of new markets such as Canada and South Africa, where the brand achieved the number one. It was at that time, 1925, that the slogan of the brand was invented: *Afore ye go* (before you leave), a kind of «spur blow», that is, before the bell rings for the game... Taking advantage of the economic recession, the company

acquired several distilleries of malt, such as Blair Athol and Dufftown and also.

The sons of Arthur Bell died in 1942, but the brand, that continued to be independent, followed its upward progression under the direction of William Govan Farquharson, who was its president until 1973. While engaged in export, the brand became the preferred of Scots in the 70s (before being defeated by The Famous Grouse), and was also number one in Britain around 1980. The Bell company was independent until 1985 when was acquired by the Guinness group, just two years before it took control of DCL to form the United Distillers group.

The main quality of the Bell's blends is the Extra Special, soft and well balanced, although there are also the eight-year-old Bell's De Luxe and the twenty-year-old Bell's Royal Reserve. Sometimes, the bottles are adorned with a golden cardboard bell, symbol of the brand.

Ben Nevis

Type: **single malt and blend.**
Origin: **Western Highlands.**
Owner: **Nikka Whisky Distilling.**
Date of birth: **1825.**

Located in Fort Williams, at the foot of the highest peak of the British Isles, the Ben Nevis that reaches 1,344 meters, the distillery of the same name was founded by the famous Long John MacDonald, who was, on the other hand, almost two meters height.

He created his famous «Dew of Ben Nevis» blend, but this brand was resold by his grandson to a London society. The distillery, however, continued within the MacDonald family for three generations and a second distillery was created to meet the demand. In addition, the arrival of the railroad, in 1894, increased its development.

After the Second World War the story of Ben Nevis was marked by another colorful character, Joseph Hobbs. He made his fortune and then ruined himself in Canada, in the 1920s, by sending liquors to the United States during prohibition. Back in Scotland, he acquired several distilleries, such as Bruichladdich and Glenkinchie, regrouped in a «Scottish Distillers Association». At the same time, he created in the Highlands, near Great Glen, a true ranch of the North America, with herds that lived as they want in those large spaces. The assistants dressed like cowboys, including the Stetson hat. In 1955, he acquired Ben Nevis, where he introduced an innovation: distilling the malt and cereal whiskies in the same place, to have the same brand for a single whisky and a blend. But it was a commercial flop and the production stopped in 1978. In 1981, the distillery returned to the same owner (Whitbread) as its original brand, Long John. The group decided to resume the distillation. But the whisky market was down and there were a lot of malts on the market, so production was suspended again in 1986.

The salvation of Ben Nevis came from abroad. It was the group Nikka, second producer of Japan, which bought the distillery in April 1989. Six months later, the production was resumed with modernized equipment, under the direction of Axel Ross, and a visitor center was inaugurated in 1991. All these adventures made Ben Nevis malts rarer, although highly appreciated by experts, for its robustness and its characteristic malted tonality. Hoping that the new productions reach a sufficient level of maturity, it is still possible to found some Ben Nevis bottlers of twelve and fifteen years of age, as well as the vintage of 1972. The distillery nowadays commercializes blends, with the brand of Long John, «Dew of Ben Nevis», in Special Reserve versions of three years of age, twelve years of age, and De Luxe, of twenty-one years of age. In addition, there are some numbered and signed bottles of a twenty-six-year-old whisky, that have a strange dark color due to their age.

An old commercial document from the Ben Nevis distillery.

Black Barrel

Type: **single grain.**
Origin: **Lowlands.**
Owner: **William Grant & Sons.**
Date of birth: **1963 (distilleries).**

For a long time, simple cereals were not marketed as such, with all production destined for blends. But the recent evolution of the market seems to indicate that there are some possibilities for development, and for this reason the group William Grant and Sons begins to propose a simple grain, baptized as Black Barrel.

It is made in the distillery of Girvan, in Ayrshire (Lowlands), one of the southernmost in Scotland. This modern facility was created in 1963 to respond to the formidable expansion of the group after the war. Apart from the cereal distillery, there is another one for malts, marketed in part under the brand Ladyburn.

The development of Black Barrel is distinguished by some details, very different from the usual process applied to malts. Only wheat is used as a raw material and a triple distillation is required to make it a satisfactory spirit. Then, aging (not specified by the producer, but at least must be three years, maybe five), is made in new oak casks, which will no longer be used for simple cereal. However, to remove roughness, these casks are flamed inside, according to the technique used in the United States for bourbons.

The set gives a soft and round whisky, very different from the usual products of Scotland. But it is an authentic whisky, light but seductive for its sweetness.

Black & White

Type: **blend.**
Origin: **Glasgow.**
Owner: **United Distillers.**
Date of birth: **1904.**

This blend, which is so well known all over the world, owes everything to the genius of one of the great figures of whisky, James Buchanan (see «Buchanan»s»). Since to make known this brand used all the resources of advertising.

At first, it was a rather light blend, without personality. But James Buchanan managed to link it to the bar of the House of Commons in London, as well as to all the theaters and cabarets in the city. He gave it a very simple look, with black letters on a white background. First sold under the name of «House of Commons» and then as Buchanans'Special, it soon became very popular, although consumers only asked for «black and white». Buchanan accepted the idea and turned it into a separate brand.

Then, he had the idea of completing the label with the association of two small terriers, the black (a Scottish dog of Aberdeen), and the white (a terrier of the west of the Highlands). The brand was launched and the black and white continued to be declined in all possible ways.

In this way, Buchanan ordered to deliver his blends throughout London by magnificent stagecoach, pulled by horses with black and white harnesses and coachmen superbly dressed.

They left every morning, without fear of the inclemencies of the time, from the central of Holborn, for the distribution in the capital. This tradition was maintained until May 1936.

These stagecoaches were a copy of the one that broke the London-Brighton record in less than eight hours. A well-loved memory for Londoners, who popularized the Black & White brand even more.

The use of black and white induced the distributor of that whisky in France to repaint in this way some Paris buses, for a great promotional operation that took place in the 80s. But the fierce opposition of the syndicates brought down this idea.

The success of the Black & White made the fortune of James Buchanan, who came to be named baron, and then Peer of the Realm.

In 1915 he partnered with Dewar to combat the growing preponderance of DCL, but in 1923 he has to retreat. Black & White and the other brands of the Buchanan group were acquired by the DCL group, today absorbed by United Distillers.

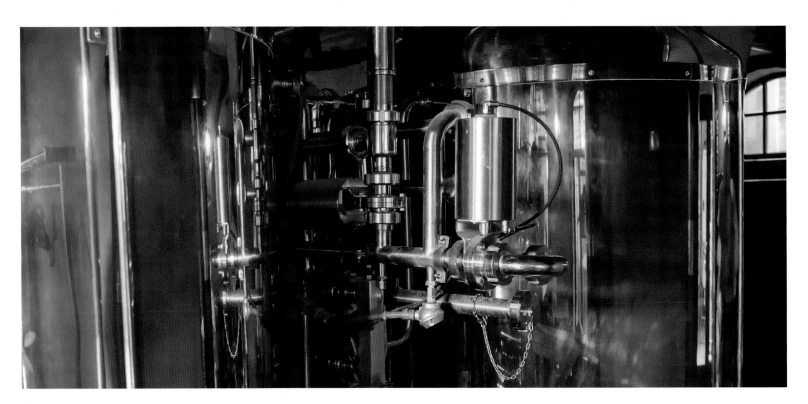

Bladnoch

Type: **single malt.**
Origin: **Lowlands (Galloway).**
Owner: **United Distillers.**
Date of birth: **1818.**

Located in the south of Scotland, on the edge of Wigtown Bay, Bladnoch is one of the rare malt distilleries of the Lowlands, and gives a perfect example of the style of malts of this region, so different from the products in the Highlands and in the islands.

Its origin is ancient, probably dating back to 1818. In this little rough rural region which, allegedly, inspire sir Walter Scott the theme of *The bride of Lammermoore,* the distillery was part of a farm and only worked in winter. It closed for the first time in the 30s, and its equipment was sold to Sweden. Re-instated after the Second World War, it changed hands several times before belonging to the Bell group in 1983, shortly before its absorption by Guinness. They decided to close it in 1993, keeping only the aging cellars. However, there is the idea of developing a visitor center and whisky museum, which already exist in the place.

The Bladnoch malt is one of those that divide the experts. For some, it is a whisky without interest, flat and not very aromatic. Others appreciate its pale color, its soft fragrance, its floral and lemon notes. Among the independent bottlers you will find a vintage of 1984, as well as very respectable versions of twenty-eight and thirty years of age. Malts of the Lowlands, like Bladnoch, possess a magnificent aptitude for very long ages.

Actually, the most current version is a ten-year-old, belonging to the series «Flora y Fauna». This range evaluates some little-known malts, associating them each time with a typical animal or plant of Scotland. For Bladnoch, it is the large-leaved hellebore, a rather rare variety of wild ranunculosa. It grows in the oak forests that surround the distillery.

The Blair Athol distillery.

Blair Athol

Type: **single malt.**
Origin: **Highlands.**
Owner: **United Distillers.**
Date of birth: **1798.**

The distillery was founded in 1798 in Pitlochry, and not in the town of Blair Atholl, fifteen kilometers further north. The quality of the water is the main reason of the installation, and there have been counted up to thirty distilleries in the area. Clear as the crystal, the stream that descends from the Ben-Y-Vrackie, has the Gaelic nickname «the river of the otter», since the presence of that mammal being a guarantee of purity.

Around 1850, P. Mackenzie & Co. bought the distillery, made several improvements and created a malting plant. Production capacities became more important (almost half a million liters a year), but it ceased in 1932. Soon after, Mackenzie passed to the Bell group, and they did not restart manufacturing until 1949, when the brand obtained its great resonance. Further improvements followed, and fortunately the oldest buildings were preserved. Recently, the entire Pitlochry region has its fortune in tourism: here you can find traditional wool shops alternating with jewelers (another Scottish artisan activity). That village is the gateway to the Highlands and its theater festival is famous.

Located at the entrance to the town, the Blair Athol distillery participates in this evolution. Apart from the fact that its malt is one of the constituents of the blend of Bell, very popular in Great Britain, the conservation of numerous old buildings has allowed to develop a true whisky information center. Very rich in objects, memories and books, it deserves a good visit to know more about the matter. The technical part is explained with extreme precision. Blair Athol's malt is very rare. It is bottled mainly twelve years old and is appreciated for its softness and its rotundity. The exclusive use of the peat in the Orkney Islands gives it a certain characteristic dryness.

Bowmore

Type: **single malt.**
Origin: **Islay.**
Owner: **Morrison-Bowmore.**
Date of birth: **1779.**

For novices who ignore everything about Islay's malts, Bowmore is undoubtedly an excellent learning experience. Well, the malts of this distillery have all the characteristics of the style of Islay so appreciated by experts, to the point that for some represents the summum of Scottish production, offering a more rounded version, less aggressive and less disconcerting for the novice.

The local situation of the distillery also counts for something. In the center of the island, in the bay protected by Lake Indaal, the town of Bowmore is often considered the «capital» of the island of Islay, despite not having more than two or three streets. It is worthy of admiration the round church, built by a French architect, so that the devil could not find a corner to settle here.

Legally, the distillery is the oldest on the island, since it was founded in 1779 by merchant Johm Simpson. But, on an isolated island, it is easy to imagine that many smugglers had, for many years before, the idea of distilling their own whisky. It knew a remarkable expansion thanks to James Mutter, who did not hesitate to go himself in search of barley and coal with his steamer, returning to land to sell his whisky. Curious-

ly, he was also consul in Glasgow of Portugal, of Brazil and of the Ottoman Empire.

Then, the distillery stopped working after the Second World War, because the facilities serve as a base to a coastal surveillance brigade. The set was acquired in 1963 by Stanley Morrison, who carried out important renovation works. However, today the malting room is preserved «on solid ground», which has the characteristic of not using too much peat, in relation to the other malts on the island. In addition, one third of the casks have contained sherry. It should be noted that part of the wineries is located below sea level. The range of whiskies marketed by Bowmore is impressive, because if you start with a ten-year-old (and there are some younger, being the Legend younger without age), you can have even a twelve years, a twenty-one years, a twenty-five years and a thirty years (bottled in 1993 for the thirtieth anniversary of the acquisition by Stanley Morrison), not forgetting the Bicentennial (surely a fifteen years old) or the Black Bowmore 1964, much rarer. This range allows to see how a whisky can evolve in so complicated ways. Having less aggressiveness than the whiskies of the south of Islay (Laphroaig or Lagavulin), and more breadth than those of the north, the whiskies of Bowmore offer with each tasting new sensations and new aromatic references. You have to discover it absolutely... before the desire to taste it often.

Brackla

Type: **single malt.**
Origin: **Highlands (Speyside).**
Owner: **United Distillers.**
Date of birth: **1812.**

This distillery proudly bears the Royal title from 1835, when King William IV granted it the «Royal Warrant of Appointment», the first title of supplier of the court obtained by a Scottish distillery.

The king liked this whisky very much, as did Queen Victoria who succeeded him, since she renewed the privilege twenty years later. But that title also owes much to the fame of the distiller, William Fraser, and his commercial spirit.

He founded his distillery in Cawdor, near Nairn, northeast of Inverness. But it was not long before he had to struggle with the competition of clandestine distillers, still numerous at the time. To differentiate himself from them, he had the idea of appealing to the Royal Commission and thus achieved an original «label». The distillery changed owners several times over

the years and was modernized in 1898. In 1926 it was taken over by John Bisset & Co., who used it mainly for the production of two blends that were very much in vogue: Bisset's Finest Old and Gold Label. Then, Brackla was absorbed by the DCL group in 1943, which modernized it several times, especially with the installation of a malting plant. But malts are only used for group blends. Only a few independent bottlers market the Royal Brackla in small quantities. The distillery closed in 1985, but in 1991 it returned to production. And then, United Distillers decided to directly market the *single malt*, emphasizing the royal privilege granted by William IV with the mention of «the king's personal whisky». It is distinguished by its characteristic fruity aromas.

Bruichladdich

Type: **single malt.**
Origin: **Islay.**
Owner: **Invergordon.**
Date of birth: **1881.**

Without being one of the oldest distilleries of Islay, Bruichladdich is undoubtedly the one that has best preserved its original appearance. It is located in front of Bowmore, next to Lake Indaal and its Gaelic name, which is pronounced in English «brewick laddie», means «shore of the coast». It is the most western distillery in all of Scotland.

It was founded by the three sons of John Harvey, a Glasgow mixer who bequeathed most of his fortune to them. But the success was not too great and the distillery, the last of the family group, closed in 1929. Run for some time by Joseph Hobbs (see «Ben Nevis»), had another period of recess before being acquired by the group Invergordon. These long periods of interruption have allowed the old-style distillery to be conserved, such as cast-iron mixing tanks, a screwed abut not-welded still, Oregon pine

At the entrance to the castle overlooking Edinburgh there is a bagpiper permanently playing the bagpipe at regular intervals.

fermentation vats, and aging cellars with clay soil. With its exterior walls painted with lime, the distillery, located on a hill overlooking the lake, can be seen from far away.

The distillation is carried out in stills with a very long neck, which gives lighter spirits than the others of Islay. In addition, the water is not extracted directly from the spring, but from a neighboring deposit, which makes it less marked by the peat than the others, since the peat is omnipresent on the island.

Bruichladdich whiskies are therefore less typified than others, but they also have great elegance, with a significant maritime presence and very subtle aromas, such as sweet almond. A very original whisky, highly exportable. The most common versions are ten, fifteen and twenty years old, but there is a twenty-five-year-old, Stillman's Dram, and the 1965 and 1969 vintages, which demonstrate once again the amazing aptitude of light whiskies for prolonged aging.

Buchanan's

Type: **blend.**
Origin: **London.**
Owner: **United Distillers.**
Date of birth: **1884.**

Great figure of the scotch whisky, of which he was one of the main promoters, James Buchanan was of modest origin; he was born in 1849, in Canada, to Scottish emigrants, who returned to Europe shortly after, and settled in Glasgow, when James was fifteen years old. James started working as a simple broker in a maritime society.

At thirty, he left for London as the representative of MacKinlay, a great merchant in wines and whiskies of the times. Only five years later, James Buchanan was on its own, borrowing from a friend and stocking whiskies for W. P. Lowrie, one of the first dealers (with Andrew Usher) to sell blends.

James Buchanan does not care about the origin because all he wants is to make blends that appeal to the people. Instead, he was an unparalleled merchant: he began distributing his bottles to all the hotels in London (which saved him from storage costs) and only charged the bottles sold once. The result of such a bold policy was immediate: in one year he had recovered all his debts and thus managed to start his commercial rise.

His greatest success was the creation of Black & White, an unprecedented marketing and advertising product, for which he created the packaging, the slogan and the emblem, the two famous black and white terriers respectively. He was also one of the first blenders to make propaganda in the press, without forgetting to get the title of provider of the court.

Lover of the horses, his colors got twice the Epsom Derby, victories that watered with rivers of whisky for all the nobility. Forerunner of sports sponsorship, he created a shooting society, the Buchanan Rifle Club, where the elite of the British army met. This dandy ended his days at the top of the social ladder, with the title of Lord Wooladington of Lavington. His power was such in the whisky world that in 1915 he partnered with Dewar to fight the DCL group, but then his business was absorbed in 1923. He ended his existence as a philanthropist in 1935, at the age of eighty-six. DCL first and United Distillers then, keep the Buchanan brand in the standard version and in the De Luxe version of twelve years of age. It obtains good results with exports, especially to the countries of South America. Dalwhinnie malt is one of its main components.

Oil painting representing the Bunnahabhain distillery.

Bunnahabhain

Type: **single malt.**
Origin: **Islay.**
Owner: **Highland Distilleries.**
Date of birth: **1881.**

It took a great courage, almost recklessness, to implant in a place as desolate as Bunnhabhian (pronounced «bu-na-ha-venn», meaning «river mouth») a distillery. Since in this region of the north of Islay there was nothing, neither a house, nor a tree, apart from an abundant spring, with water of good quality. All the material had to be transported by boat, since no road or path led to such a place.

Such obstacles did not prevent the Greenles brothers from carrying out their daring enterprise. These farmers knew that their barley transformed into whisky would assure them an excellent income. At that time, in fact, the exceptional growth of the blends market needed more and more malts, and those of Islay were almost the most appreciated, together with those of the Campbeltown region. It took only two years, from 1881 to 1883, to build the whole installation, organized around a square courtyard. Numerous incidents enameled the works,

among which a formidable storm that ruined part of the construction, half finished, and sank two ships. A narrow and winding road was built next to the nearest port and even a school, which made Bunnahabhain an acceptable village.

In 1887, the company of the Greenles brothers merged with that of Glen Rothes, constituting the Highland Distilleries, a society that remains independent.

The malt of Bunnahabhain is quite different from the other Malts of Islay, although it shares its same iodized taste, not to say maritime.

The use of peat is much more limited in malting and the stills are huge, bulbous. During distillation, the retained cup is much smaller than others. Aging takes place in casks of sherry and bourbon and lasts twelve years before bottling, in cellars that are at natural temperature: cold in winter and cool in summer.

These techniques give a whisky much lighter than other products of the region, but with a specific softness, very elegant, and of great freshness. The marine aromas are very marked, and the flavor is remarkable. For almost a century, all the production of the distillery was reserved for the mixers, and only since the 1960s some of the production begin to be commercialized in bottles.

The current presentation dates from 1979, with a dark and squat bottle, an illustration representing a Scottish sailor and the mention «Westering Home», which is the beginning of a very popular Scottish song, which describes the love of the inhabitants of the west of the Highlands for their islands. There is only one variety of Bunnahabhain whisky, twelve years old, bottled at 40^c after a slow reduction.

AND ALSO...

Balmenach
This distillery of Speydide, in Cromdale, was at the beginning of the 19th century a farm where James MacGregor distilled clandestinely. Becoming official, Balmenach knew many avatars in the twentieth century. Closed during the two wars, it became the property of the DCL group. Then, a storm destroyed the chimneys in 1979, miraculously avoiding the fire. His whisky, powerful and floral at the same time, is very appreciated by experts, but the distillery has not been working since 1993.

Banff
Founded in 1824 in the town of the same name and displaced forty years later to Inverboyndie, the distillery has been mostly used for blends. A fire destroyed it in 1877, then a bomb destroyed it partly in 1941. Owned by DCL, it produced a whisky for the House of Commons before closing in 1983.

Begg
Created by the distiller of the same name, installed not far from Mount Lochnagar, this blend has known international fame at the beginning of the century. Re-installed in 1916 by DCL, it is still seen in some markets, such as Germany and Madeira.

Beneagles
This brand of blend created in 1922 in Perth, by Peter Thompson, was long famous in Scotland for its yellow delivery vans. It also served to decorate ceramic miniatures, very sought after by collectors.

Ben Riach
Created in 1897, north of Speyside, the distillery closed six years later, reopening in... 1965. Seagram enlarged and modernized it, especially for the production of Chivas Regal. The bottling of whisky is very recent.

Benrinnes
This distillery of Speyside dates from 1826. Passed to the DCL group in 1925, was modernized and greatly expanded in 1955. Serving first of all the elaboration of the Crawford blends, the bottling of the whisky only dates from 1991. It has a partial, unusual distillation, in three stages.

Benromach
Founded in 1898 in Speyside (in the Findhorn region), it had many owners (with the famous Joseph Hobbs

among them) and different production stops before joining the DCL group in 1955. Judged excessively small and without deserving renewal, it closed in 1983. Its whisky is available among some independent bottlers.

Black Bottle
Although created in 1897, that is more than a century ago, this quality blend has been famous in Scotland only a few years. This is undoubtedly due to its moderate price. Today belongs to the group Allied Domecq.

Black Prince
Created in the 50s, this brand of blend was acquired in 1991 by Burn Stewart, who redid his packaging in three different versions (standard, twelve years of age and pottery vase), for export, especially to the Far East. The mark refers to the Black Prince (1330-1376), son of Edward III, who distinguished himself during the battle of Poitiers, coated in a dark armor.

Braes of Glenlivet
This modern distillery was created in the 70s. Founded by Seagram, it is essentially destined for the production of Chivas Regal. There are some bottles available among the independents.

Bulloch Lade's (B-L)
This blend of the United Distillers group is remarkably linked with the Caol Ila malt. It is only intended for export, especially to Canada, the United States and New Zealand.

Burberry's
Launched by Burn Stewart, this brand refers to the house of British garments (the famous trenches). Its label bears the motif of one of the most famous fabrics in the world.
There are several references of luxury blends, with a twelve-year-old and a fifteen-year-old.

Cameron Brig

Type: **single grain.**
Origin: **Lowlands.**
Owner: **United Distillers.**
Date of birth: **1824.**

Caol Illa

Type: **single malt.**
Origin: **Islay.**
Owner: **United Distillers.**
Date of birth: **1846.**

John Haig was only twenty-one years old when he built the Cameronbridge distillery, in Markinch, Fife. But he had one reason: one of his ancestors already had a reputation as a distiller in 1655. At the beginning it was a malts distillery, but John Haig soon became interested in the invention of one of his cousins, Robert Stein: continuous distillation, tone-up in 1827. As the price of cereals had dropped much, John was the first to install stills and distill only grain, mainly wheat.

John Haig was thus able to take full advantage of the expansion of the blends, and in the 1870s, Cameronbridge already produced about 5.5 million liters, which was fabulous for the time.

At the end of his life, John Haig was the artisan who regroup the grain distilleries within the Distillers Company Limited, which would become the large group of whisky producers. His successors then left the DCL, but then returned to it in 1919. Since then, the Cameronbridge distillery has not stopped growing and modernizing. Its production was interrupted only in World War II when restrictions also reached cereals. Today it is one of the most modern distilleries in Europe.

Traditionally, Cameronbrige always bottled a small part of its single grain production, and for a long time was the only one to do so. Its brand -Old Cameron Brig- is sold mainly in Scotland, especially in the Edinburgh region. It is a fairly colored whisky and much less light than would be expected from a single grain. It has aromas of plants, with a slightly spicy character.

The Caol Ila distillery.

Cardhu

Type: **single malt.**
Origin: **Highlands (Speyside).**
Owner: **United Distillers.**
Date of birth: **1824.**

In a cove near Port Askaig, the main port for ferries on the island of Islay, the distillery of Caol Ila (pronounced «cull cela» meaning «Strait of Islay»), goes back to 1846, founded by a certain Hector Henderson who had already trained at the Littlemill distillery.

The water comes from Lake Nam Ban, less than two kilometers from the distillery, and runs through the peat bogs before falling through a waterfall of beautiful effect. In the past it served both as a raw material for whisky and as a source of energy for the entire company.

As wanted by the Victorian tradition, the builders of the distillery had to add not only accommodation for the workers but also a church, used until 1930 with officiants from Glasgow or Edinburgh. Caol Ila resumed production in 1857 by Bulloch Lade, who created a landing dock at the foot of the distillery, and the vapors carried the barley there in one direction and took the casks of whisky in the other. But currently, all traffic is carried out by Port Askaig. In 1927, the company became a subsidiary of the DCL group. From 1972, a total reconstruction was carried out in two years. All the buildings were restored, the stills were changed and only the cellars were kept. The distillery has lost in character but has gained in efficiency.

The malts of Caol Ila no have never been marketed as such, except in very small quantities. With difficulty it is possible to find a twelve-year-old Bulloch Lade or fifteen years in the series «Flora and Fauna», and a few vintages among the independent bottlers. However, the experts are delighted with the greasy, peaty character and the wide aromatic range of that single malt. Clear and quite light, it is very marked by marine notes.

Caol Ila malt is one of the components of five-year-old vatted malt (or pure malt) marketed by Bulloch Lade under the name of Glen Ila. Sold mainly in the export, and especially in Italy, develops the peat aroma of Caol Ila, easy to identify.

As in many distilleries in the region, the history of Cardhu began in hiding. John Cumming, who settled on a farm at the foot of some hills where several sources flow, had several dislikes with the authorities by illicit distillation. His wife, Helen, did everything she could to help him. It was she who received the region tax men, invited them to eat and then warned the whole region about such a presence raising a flag on top of the farm. All the smugglers of the sector only had to disguise their work, waiting for better occasions.

Finally, John Cumming got an official license as a distiller and his activity was continued by his son, Lewis, and then by his wife, Elizabeth, in 1872. She was a very remarkable business woman and knew how to guide and develop the company, earning the nickname «Queen of the whisky trade».

Understanding the great future that was offered to her with the development of malts, she built a new distillery, reaching a production of about 200,000 liters.

So good business naturally interested a large number of groups of distillers, but Elizabeth stood firm for twenty years, before yielding to the offer of John Walker&Sons (Johnnie Walker). She imposed a condition: her son would continue in business and run the Cardhu distillery. This was accepted, and later her grandson Ronald became one of the leaders of the company, already acquired by the DCL group. Once bottled under the name of «Cardow» or «Cardhu», the malt became at the beginning of the century one of the basic ingredients of the Johnnie Walker Red Label and Black Label. And in view of its success, all production quickly became said ingredient. It was in the 60's when the twelve-year-old Cardhu was again marketed in a bottle of soft and rounded shapes that remind the women who contributed to its development. Whisky is sometimes described as feminine by its tasters. In any case it is an excellent blend, round and well dissolved, and is suitable for a first approach to Speyside malts by neophytes.

The distillery of Cardhu makes a malt for Johnnie Walker.

Chivas Regal

Type: **blend.**
Origin: **Highlands.**
Owner: **Seagram.**
Date of birth: **1909.**

Tourist map of a part of Speyside, with its distilleries and rivers that are characterized by their salmon.

The bottles of the best-known luxury blend in the whole world bear the date of 1801, but the brand did not appear until a century later. Actually, this date corresponds to the creation in Aberdeen of a small commerce of wines and groceries by William Edward. At that time, the port of North Scotland was in full growth and all kinds of merchandise flowed into it: tea, coffee, spices, rum, gin, wines, etc. The first Chivas, James, appeared in 1837, when William Edward was trying to develop his wine and liquor business, which he had installed on a beautiful street in the center of the city. The Chivas family was well known in the Aberdeen region, their ancestors being the barons of Schivas.

In spite of the death of William Edward in 1841, the commerce prospered and ob-

tained an increasingly aristocratic clientele. Queen Victoria, who often rested in her castle in Balmoral, in the Highlands, especially during summer vacations, made purchases in Chivas home, later giving it the title of official supplier since 1843. The quality of the products and services of Chivas was increasingly appreciated, even abroad, having also the Emperor of Austria as a customer of whiskies.

In 1858, James associated the company with his brother John and the business took the name of Chivas Brothers. Whisky became an increasingly important activity, and Chivas launched its own brand of blend around 1870, the Glen Dee, having among its clientele numerous personalities from all social classes: aristocrats, military, religious and teachers. When John died in 1863,

James took his son Alexandre as his successor, but he and his wife died in 1893, leading to the extinction of the Chivas lineage.

The trade, however, continued with Alexandre Smith, assistant to Alexandre Chivas, and then under the direction of Stewart Howard, an experienced professional in the whisky business. At the end of the century, the main brands of Chivas, Royal Glen Dee and Royal Strathythan, were well known, with an excellent image of quality in the best environments. The activity of the retail trade continued although it no longer occupied more than a very secondary part.

Following the policy of the Chivas, Stewart Howard constituted important storages of quality whisky, and to prevail in the American and Canadian markets, created around 1909 the Chivas Regal, a luxury whisky of great quality. Between the two wars there were many problems in the company Chivas. In 1929, Aberdeen's main warehouse was destroyed in part by a fire; then, in 1935, Alexandre Smith and Stewart Howard died at the same time. And finally, the war ended export activities.

But the Chivas brand retained all its prestige. Samuel Bronfman, the PDG of the powerful Canadian Seagram spirits company, who had wanted to be owner in Scotland in the past, acquired Chivas in 1949. Soon after, he bought the Strathisla distillery, opened another one in Keith, and an important complex of bottling.

The global company of Seagram turned Chivas Regal into a great international brand. The luxury blend saw its composition improved, using some of the best Speyside malts, with a minimum of twelve years of age. Soft and well structured, Chivas Regal was already a reference for those who wanted a quality whisky.

Long before the current success of simple whiskies, Chivas demonstrated to consumers around the world that Scotch whisky is not limited to standard blends of three or five years of age. Chivas markets other blends: 100 Pipers, light and very floral; Passport, pale and of frank taste; Royal Salute, twenty-one years old, the superior version of the Chivas Regal, of great harmony and very melted, with a rich aromatic range that makes it an exceptional blend.

Clan Campbell

Type: **blend.**
Origin: **Highlands.**
Owner: **Campbell Distillers (Pernod-Ricard).**
Date of birth: **1983.**

Today there must be about 14 million of Campbell in the world, all related to one of the oldest clans in Scotland. This last name appeared already in the eleventh century, on the occasion of the marriage of Gillespic Cambel (or Campbell) with the daughter of the last of the Duin, who belonged to the mythical clan of the Diarmid.

The clan had its great hero, Colin Campbell, who died in 1294, during the Battle of Methven defending the King of Scotland against the English invader. In his memory, the leader of the Campbell clan always held the title of Mac Cailein Mor, «son of the Great Colin» in Gaelic.

Associated with all the phases of the history of Scotland, the Campbells adopted in 1457 the title of Counts of Argyll (later, Dukes from 1701) and created the village of Inveraray, where the family castle still stands, rebuilt from 1746. The second Duke was associated with the Act of Union between Scotland and England. The eighth Duke was a minister for twenty years in the 19th century and one of his sons married a daughter of Queen Victoria.

The bonds of the Campbells with the whisky are less known, although 1563 is a key date: Mary Stuart, Queen of Scotland, visiting her sister the Countess of Argyll, tasted the whisky of the clan. And the Campbells have always drunk a whisky to her health.

The commercial company House of Campbell was officially created in Glasgow in 1879, but the true start of the Clan Campbell blend only dates back to 1983. The Pernod-Ricard group, king of a very delicate anise, acquired the Campbell brand from the twelfth Duke of Argyll, Sir Ian Douglas, who already owned the distilleries of Edradour and Aberlour. The Duke, gentleman farmer and businessman, is part of the board of directors of Campbell Distillers.

The commercial strength of the French group in Europe has made Clan Campbell a huge success in ten years, being that blend the third brand in the hexagonal market. All communication focuses on the prestigious past of the clan and the history of Scotland. The distillery of Glenallachie, created by Mackinlays in 1967, and closed in the early

1980s, was acquired by the Campbell Distillers group in 1989 to meet its malt needs.

Next to the Campbell Clan blend appears instantly the twenty-one years old, the Legendary (in 1987) and twelve years old, the Highlander (1992). All three are well balanced, in the Speyside style. In addition, the group also produces the White Heather, an eight-year-old blend, distributed mainly in France in the café-restaurant circuit.

Clynelish

Type: **single malt.**
Origin: **Northern Highlands.**
Owner: **United Distillers.**
Date of birth: **1819.**

The first distillery installed in 1819 in this area in the Northern Highlands was named Brora. Its founder, the Duke of Sutherland, had dumped several thousand farmers and their families from their lands in order to develop lamb farming, which was more profitable. The villagers emigrated en masse to the more fertile Brora region, and to produce the harvested barley, the duke built this distillery. At the same time, he wanted to defeat the numerous clandestine distillers in the region. To secure its energy needs the exploitation of a nearby coal deposit was attempted, but it lacked the necessary qualities.

In 1896, the distillery passed into the hands of James Ainslie, a wine merchant who became a mixer, but the era was bad for whisky and Brora finally joined the DCL group in 1925. The brand of Ainslie's blends (standard and luxury) has been preserved by United Distillers, although it is not widespread.

In 1967, a new distillery was built nearby, with the name of Clynelish. Then, the old one was definitively closed in the 80s.

Among the independent bottlers are still whiskies of the old Brora distillery, especially the vintage of 1972. Clynelish whisky is a twelve-year-old highly appreciated by experts, although little bottled. The maritime position of the distillery gives it special iodine aromas, as well as a great strength, which makes possible to compare it with a whisky from the islands.

Cragganmore

Type: **single malt.**
Origin: **Highlands (Speyside).**
Owner: **United Distillers.**
Date of birth: **1869.**

The founder of this distillery was at the time one of the best specialists in the field of whisky. John Smith, in fact, had directed Macallan, The Glenlivet, Wishaw and, Glenfarclas, where he convinced his superior to help him create a new distillery.

Its location, at the confluence of the Spey and Avon rivers, was deliberately chosen to take advantage of the proximity of the new railway line. For this reason, a small train reminiscent of that railway origin can be seen on the current label of the bottle. On the other hand, numerous springs well up on the hill behind the buildings. The stills have an unusual shape, with a rather flat neck.

Lover of the railroads, John Smith had difficulty living his passion. He was so fat (over 140 kilos) that he could not get into the wagons and he had to travel on the conductor platform.

When he died, in 1886, the distillery passed to his son Gordon, who expanded and modernized it in 1901. Then, in 1923, it was bought by the White Horse group, which entered in 1965 in the DCL group.

For a long time, the Cragganmore malt was used almost exclusively by the blenders, especially for the elaboration of McCallum's&Perfection blends (named after two business brothers in Edinburgh). These blends were very popular in Australia, but in 1989, the makers of the United Distillers group decided to choose them to represent Speyside in their «Classic Malts», range, which led Cragganmore out of unjustified ignorance.

A bit austere, the twelve-year-old whisky reveals an incredible complexity of aromas and flavors, amplified by aging in sherry casks. Of a beautiful golden color, it is pleasantly net and balanced, and of a superb duration.

The independent bottlers propose other versions, among which one vintage of 1976 not reduced, to 53,8°, and another of 1974.

Cutty Sark

Type: **blend.**
Origin: **London.**
Owner: **Berry Bros & Rudd.**
Date of birth: **1923.**

The whisky is not only related to distillers and merchants but also to myths and legends throughout Scotland, of which Cutty Sark is an admirable example. The same name is owed to a comic poem, «Tam O'Shanter», written in the 18th century by Robert Burns, referring to a young and pretty sorceress, dressed in a «short shirt» *(cutty sark,* in Scottish). The sorceress pursues a farmer who has surprised a meeting of witches in a cemetery, but he escapes and only remains in the hands of the sorceress the tail of the farmer's horse.

Cutty Sark, the sorceress of light foot, is an essential figure in all the Scottish legends. Thus, in 1869, when the shipyards of Dumbarton launched a new clipper very fast, its owners naturally gave it her name. The ship met a very surprising career, first carrying out the tea trade in the China Sea, then developed innumerable links between London and the Empire. In 1887 it made the feat of uniting Australia with England in sixty-nine days, a record that nobody matched at the time. Then it became the ship-school of the British Merchant Marine, before finishing its days in Greenwich, where it is still a tourist attraction, with more than half a million visitors each year.

The route of the Cutty Sark joined the whisky on March 23, 1923, in the superb hall of the leaders of Berry Bros, at No. 3 of St. James Street, London. These respectable wine and liquor merchants, whose business went back to 1690, want equally dedicate themselves to the whisky industry and launch a new blend. Present at the meeting, James Mac Bey, famous Scottish artist, suggested the name «Cutty Sark», and drew the label as well as its topography, reproducing the famous clipper, accompanied by the mention «Scots whisky», while others were called scotch whisky. The background was supposed to be ocher color but, due to a printer error, a canary yellow was used, so surprising that it was immediately adopted. To seduce the American clientele, Berry

The *Cutty Sark* was one of the fastest sailboats in the world.

Bros chose a light and very clear blend, prefiguring the dominant trend of the development of the blends for the second half of the century.

The legend of Cutty Sark does not end in such a good way. In effect, there is another figure: the smuggler captain William McCoy. Installed in the Bahamas, he was one of the first to want to challenge the prohibition that had existed since 1920 in the United States. And unlike the gangsters, he categorically refused to deliver counterfeit liquors, so he continued to give his customers «authentic» products. This image has remained impressed in the minds of consumers, because today, in North American bars, the name McCoy still stands for authenticity.

After his relationship with Francis Berry, the Cutty Sark blend was one of his pilot products. McCoy contributed to make it an international brand of great fame, and it's still like that.

Apart from the standard blend, Cutty Sark proposes versions of twelve and eighteen years of age.

AND ALSO...

Caperdonich

This distillery is the twin sister of Glen Grant, in Rothes, on Speyside, built directly opposite. Use the same water, the same malt and the same distillation techniques. And yet, the two whiskies are very different! Essentially used for blends (mostly Chivas Regal), whisky is available among some independent bottlers.

Catto's

This brand of blend was created in Aberdeen, in 1861, and had a rapid international progress thanks to the emigrants of the region. Today belongs to the Inver House group.

Chieftain's Choice

Under this name a vast range of blends and high quality single malts are grouped, all belonging to the Peter Russell group, one of the most important independent companies in the market, founded in 1936. It was acquired in 1985 by the Scottish Independent Distillers Company and distributes its high-quality whiskies thanks to a network of specialized merchants.

Claymore

Launched by DCL in 1977, this brand of blend was originally a «second prize», destined to face the provisional withdrawal of Johnnie Walker from the British market. Then, before the alleged cartel against DCL, the brand was sold, like others, to Whyte&MacKay. Today, it is in the squad of the ten best-selling brands in the United Kingdom.

Cluny

Referring to MacPhersons de Cluny, one of the companions of the Scottish hero Bonnie Prince Charles, this blend (standard and luxury versions) was created in 1857 by one of the descendants of that one. Belonging to the Invergordon group, it is a brand only dedicated today to export to North America, as well as to some European countries.

Coleburn

Installed since 1896 near the city of Elgin, this Speyside distillery has provided a lot of malt for the elaboration of the Usher's blend, and also for the Johnnie Walker.
Owned by DCL since 1930, it retains its original appearance, despite the work that has been done in it over the years. It has been in recess since 1985, but some vintage whiskies (especially of 1972) can still be found among the independent bottlers.

Convalmore

Installed in Dufftown (Speyside) in 1894, this distillery provided malts for the Grant's blend. After a fire in 1909, a new process of continuous distillation of malt whisky, similar to that used for single grain, was installed. But it was abandoned, since the aging of this brandy did not give good results. Owned by the United Distillers group, the distillery closed in 1985. A few vintages are available among independent bottlers.

Craigellachie

Located at the confluence of the Fiddich and Spey rivers, the village of Craigellachie is a road junction between the A9 and the road that leads to Dufftown. Founded in 1898 by Peter Mackie, the distillery was mainly used to make the White Horse blend, whose name is proudly seen on its walls, after its reconstruction in 1965. Whisky is only available in the «Flora and Fauna» series and among some independent bottlers.

Crawford's

This brand of blend very popular in Scotland dates back to the brothers Archibald and Aikman Crawford, whisky traders in Leith around 1860. The label has not changed since 1900, and the brand belongs to the United Distillers group since 1944, although it was exploited by Whyte&Mackay since 1986 in the United Kingdom. It is also exported to countries such as Italy, Holland and South Africa.

Dalmore

Type: **single malt.**
Origin: **Northern Highlands.**
Owner: **Whyte&Mackay.**
Date of birth: **1839.**

Founded in 1839, near Alness, the distillery benefits from a superb location on the edge of Cromarty Bay, facing Noire Island. The port activities are old there, especially in transport of wood for the construction of boats. Surrounded by mountains that exceed 600 meters in altitude, Morie Lake supplies the Alness River, and the distillery has exclusive water for its needs. If the founder left few memories, much more is known about those who bought it in 1867, the Mackenzie brothers, some farmers of the region, since their family has kept the agenda in which the daily activity was recorded. This precious testimony shows especially the important role played by whisky in the local economy, both for the use of barley and for the financial contribution that its sale represents.

The Mackenzie family retained ownership of Dalmore until 1960, the date of its merger with the Whyte&Mackay group. But the two societies had many ties of friendship and commercial collaboration for many years, so there is always some Mackenzie in the group.

Despite the strike during the First World War, which forced a profound restructuring in 1922, Dalmore has retained much of its original aspect. One of its stills dates from 1874, and all have a special form, very stubby, with a very short swan neck, although they are of different sizes.

The architecture and decoration of the building are reminiscent of an old station and inside there are coatings and oak coffered ceilings from a hunting lodge. There is still the railway platform, which perhaps explains why Dalmore was one of the first malts to be bottled and commercialized, since the expeditions were facilitated by the railroad.

Aging is largely ensured by the bourbon casks, and the rest is placed in casks of sherry (fragrant) and the final blend is made in large casks of sherry

Dalmote's whisky is eight years old (an unusual thing), although there are also twelve and eighteen ones. Little known, that single malt is nevertheless something superb. Little peaty, it is especially sweet, with fruity aromas and very interesting cereals, as well as a long duration.

Dalwhinnie

Type: **single malt.**
Origin: **Highlands (Speyside).**
Owner: **United Distillers.**
Date of birth: **1898.**

The Dalwhinne Distillery is next to the main road that runs through the Highlands.

Deanston

Type: **single malt.**
Origin: **Highlands.**
Owner: **Burn Stewart.**
Date of birth: **1965.**

Lying 327 meters above the sea, Dalwhinnie is the Scottish distillery with the highest altitude. It is located at a strategic crossroads between the north-south and east-west axes that connect the different regions of the Higlands. The climate is rigorous and the site is often isolated by snow. However, there is an abundance of river water, and peat bogs are strongly present throughout the area.

Cattle drivers, rival armies and whisky smugglers crossed over there over the centuries, and thus, dalwhinnie means in Gaelic «meeting point».

Even parts of the road built by General Wade in the eighteenth century to better control militarily the Highlands, which were in almost constant rebellion against the government of London, still exist near the construction.

However, it was not until the end of the 19th century that the distillery (originally named Strathspey) was built by two partners from Kingussie, a few kilometers away. But the business went from bad to worse and the facilities were resold in 1905 to a North American company, Cook&Bernheimer. This alarmed the Scottish distillers, disturbed by this intrusion into their territories.

But the US prohibition calmed their fears and Dalwhinnie was acquired again in 1926 by DCL, under the control of James Buchanan. The malt, rarely bottled, except for local consumption, was then one of the basic ingredients of the Black&White blend. The distillery received the visitors in a center where the history of James Buchanan was widely exposed. The buildings were largely devastated by a fire in 1934 and the distillery did not function again until 1938. The place, isolated and wild, deserves to be visited before reaching Speyside.

Since 1988, Dalwhinnie whisky has entered the range of the «Classics Malts» of the United Distillers group, which ensures a well-deserved wide spread. Although the distillery is located more than 40 kilometers from the River Spey, it is related to Speyside whiskies. The fifteen years of age, most available, is quite clear, which does not mean it is light. But its power is not overwhelming, as justified by its nickname of «gentle spirit». Very aromatic, has fruity and honey notes, and offers a very soft structure. A whisky that knows how to disguise his play.

Located in Doune, on the border between the Highlands and the Lowlands, this distillery is quite recent, although the buildings it occupies date back to 1785. It was a cotton spinning mill, created by Richard Arkwright, one of the inventors of the first workshops of mechanical spinning, at the beginning of the Industrial Revolution.

Nearby are the picturesque ruins of the medieval castle of Doune. The spinning mill existed until 1960, and was converted into malt distillery in 1965. The two industries, in fact, have several points in common, especially in water feeding, provided in abundant quantity by the Teith River. Regarding the vast warehouses of cotton storage, they are very suitable for the aging of the whisky in casks, since they were conceived to maintain a constant temperature and hygrometry. However, three intermediate floors had to be removed in order to house four stills.

These arrangements were made by Brodie Hepburn, specialist in the whisky business. In 1972 the distillery became the property of the Invergordon group, during a good period for the whisky market, but closed for long time in the 80s, until it was finally acquired by Burn Stewart in 1991.

This company, specializing in blends, markets Deanston malts, available in several versions: twelve, seventeen and twenty-five years. Although the place officially belongs to the Highlands, this whisky rather belongs to the lowlands, being pale and light, soft, slightly malted, with a very sweet, somewhat fruity finish.

Defender

Type: **blend.**
Origin: **Glasgow.**
Owner: **Dalaruan.**
Date of birth: **1989.**

The «defender» designates in a combat who defends his title against a rival. This is the symbol adopted by seven houses of wines and spirits from around the world to create a brand of blends capable of competing with the great world groups. Such is in any case the ambition of Defender, which appeared at the end of the 80s.

The constituent companies of the group - Robertson & Baxter of Glasgow, owner of the Glengoyne distillery; Asbach spirits in Germany; Pescarmona in Italy; Ports and Sherry of Osborne; the Plantes Reunis of Switzerland; Takahashi of Japan; Chaitre Taittinger de France-, have as points in common to be family structures and to be independent. Distributing reciprocally most of their products, they wanted to have with this brand a weapon to better develop internationally, especially in the United States and Japan, because whisky is still one of the most profitable liquors today. The label reproduces a world map.

Owned in equal parts by the seven founders, Defender has also adopted the Dalaruan banner, one of Campbeltown's numerous distilleries that existed in the last century. It was founded in 1824 by a certain Charles Colvill, but it disappeared like many others during the North American prohibition, since it had specialized in supplying the American market. Today there are only two distilleries left in Campbeltown, against more than thirty a hundred and fifty years ago.

The Defender five years of age is a blend made of about twenty-five different whiskies, of which a third at least are single malts, mostly from the Highlands. It is an amber whisky, fairly balanced, with good smoothness.

Since its birth, the Defender brand still have two other qualities: the Defender Success, a twelve year old presented in a bottle inspired by the great brands of perfume; The Defender Very Classic Palé, very clear, that follows the recent fashion of blond and light whiskies, very appreciated in the discotheques of the whole world.

About the Defender, the novelist Bernard Franck wrote: «Whisky can allow you to victoriously resist the hashes of heaven and luck. Defender, yes, the word is correct and Churchillian, and the product is as frank as the word. I dream of Montesquieu, who affirmed that he knew no evil that would resist an hour of reading. Less romantic than him, I add to this pleasure a little of this fire spirit».

Dewar's

Type: **blend.**
Origin: **Perth.**
Owner: **United Distillers.**
Date of birth: **1860.**

Following a great Scottish tradition, the founder of one of the most sold brands of whisky in the world has very modest origins. In 1828, at the age of twenty-three, John Dewar left his small town of Moneydie on foot to work in Perth, 40 kilometers away, in the wine and liquor store of a close relative. It took him nine years to become a business partner and, in 1846, he opened his own business in Perth, on the High Street, where he started selling his blends.

At the end of the 1860s, John Dewar had the idea of selling his products in bottles with his brand and not in casks or clay jars, as was customary at that time.

At his death, in 1880, his two sons, John Alexander and Thomas Robert, resumed the business, which they gave an incredible development. They were very different. Thomas, the youngest, was worldly, extroverted and knew how to innovate at every moment, John was more austere, directing almost only the finances of society and hardly leaving his native Scotland.

Therefore, it was Thomas who settled in London in 1885 to open a branch. He did so much for his brand as well as for the knowledge of whisky in general, that he earned the nickname «Whisky Tom». Joined the upper classes, was familiar with the future Edward VII and Thomas Lipton, the king of spices. With them, he was one of the first British to own a car. On one of his business cards he wrote: « I stopped lending money a long time ago. But I still like to drink. Make it is a Dewar's».

His work and his social skills allowed him to place the Dewar's White Label in all the fashionable places. Accompanying his commercial talent was a great sense of publicity. On the occasion of a great fair of farmers and brewers, in 1896, he brought to his stand a bagpipe player, with ceremonial dress, which surprised more than one visitor. He was inspired by the idea of the Highlander (inhabitant of the Highlands) in the form of a giant flag to illuminate a building in London on the banks of the Thames, admired by all Londoners. Thomas Dewar was also a great traveler, visiting more than twenty-six countries between 1892 and 1894, hiring thirty-two agents and opening an office in New York, in 1895. Meanwhile, his brother created bottling plants in London and Manchester, and he set up a malt distillery in Aberfeldy, in order to secure supplies. Six others followed, created or acquired as second-hand: Lochnagar, Ord, Pulteney, Aultmore, Parkmore and Benrinnes. Both brothers were ennobled by his merits. John was the first in the world of whisky to be a baron, in 1907, then Peer of the Realm, as Lord Forteviot. His brother Thomas acceded to the title of Baron Dewar of Homestall in 1919 and carried out important functions in the city council of London. The two brothers died a year apart, in 1929 and 1930. However, the business continued to expand, first under the direction of Peter Dewar (namesake with no family ties to the founders), then under that of the founder's grandson, John Arthur, and finally with his cousin Evelyn.

Previously, Dewar had been associated with James Buchanan since 1915. A very beneficial union as the two societies once owned the largest stock of whiskeys in Scotland. But the group had to join the DCL in 1925.

The Dewar brand continued its rise, taking full advantage of the end of the prohibition in the United States, where it became number one in whisky sales.

It is distributed in more than one hundred and forty countries, which has earned him several times the great royal prize of export: «The Queen's Award».

Dimple

Type: **blend.**
Origin: **Lowlands.**
Owner: **United Distillers.**
Date of birth: **1893.**

The history of this luxury blend brand is closely linked to that of John Haig and his descendants. Made from about thirty different whiskies, with the Lowlands Glenkinchie malt, it extracts its originality from the shape of the bottle, imagined in 1893 by George Ogilvy Haig. With a triangular structure, it has a rounded silhouette.

This original and without precedents drawing got the fortune of the brand in the export, especially in the United States, where they gave it the nickname of «Pinch», better known than the name Dimple. It became the workhorse of the exporting society of Alicius Haig. This bottle was conceived for the luxury version of the Haig blend. The name «Dimple Scots» appeared in 1912 and it was not until the 20s that the «Dimple» mark was used.

The bottle offers another particularity: is surrounded by a fine wire net. Originally, it served to maintain the cork that closed the container, so that it could withstand without damage the movement of the navigation. Since the cap was replaced by a capsule, this protection is already useless, but it is so identified with the brand that it was conserved. This net is manufactured in Spain and France, then placed in the bottling workshop of Markinch, Scotland, a costly operation that cannot be mechanized. The popularity of this original bottle is unparalleled. Thus, it serves as a container for miniature ships for numerous model makers. It was also the favorite bank for millions of children around the world who kept their coins in it. It is, finally, the first bottle that was the subject of a legal deposit in the United States, in 1958, in order to limit piracy increasingly booming. Whisky, on the other hand, is a harmonious blend, well dissolved and of beautiful duration. Marketed once of twelve years, now it has fifteen years old (in any case, in the European market), a little richer in flavor. Its great originality depends on a lowland malt, the Glenkinchie, especially round and slightly smoked, although in total about thirty different whiskies are in the final blend.

Dufftown

Type: **single malt.**
Origin: **Highlands (Speyside).**
Owner: **United Distillers.**
Date of birth: **1895.**

Of the seven distilleries that make Dufftown one of the capitals of Speyside, or of Scotch whisky, this is the only one to hold such a name. Interestingly, the mention «Glenlivet», was added to it, when the river of the same name runs away from there. And for some tasters, the style of their malts does not resemble it at all. It is useless to try to understand it! The Lord of Fife, Alexander Duff of Braco, gave his name to the town of Dufftown when he acquired Balvenie Castle, in 1673.

The creation of the distillery goes back to the end of the 19th century: two merchants from Liverpool, Peter Mackenzie and Richard Stackpole, bought a mill located not far from the distillery of Mortlach. In 1895 it was transformed into a distillery, with an assured supply of barley thanks to the vicinity of the Pittyvaich farm. The water comes from a spring, the Jock's Well, famous in the region for its quality and abundance, whose owners had difficulty securing exclusivity. The company Mackenzie had a very important development at the beginning of the 20th century, acquiring other distilleries, among which Blair Athol, and increased its sales in the North American market until the time of the prohibition. It was merged in 1933 with the Bell group, which made Dufftown one of its basic malts. Despite grain restrictions during World War II, Dufftown never stopped its production. In 1968, the distillery doubled its production capacity, and ten years later two new stills were installed, allowing it to produce a total of more than 27 million liters a year. In 1985, like the Bell group, Dufftown was absorbed by United Distillers.

Like the eight-year-old, Dufftown whiskies are quite light, a blend of smoke and malt. There is a version of ten years and another of fifteen, in the series «Flora and Fauna».

AND ALSO...

Dailuaine

This distillery of Speyside was founded in 1851 by William Mackenzie, and benefited from the proximity of the railway. Later it became part of the DCL group, becoming one of the malts that enters the composition of the Johnnie Walker. Single malt, very aromatic with marked notes of sherry, is only available in the sixteen-year-old version of «Flora and Fauna», and in a few vintages among independent bottlers.

Dallas Dhu

Founded in 1899 in Speyside, this distillery is not of American origin, as the translation of its name into Gaelic means «black water valley». After having several owners, it joined the DCL group in 1923.

Interrupted by a fire in 1939, production was maintained until the beginning of the 1980s, the date of final closure. But the place and the historical character of its buildings have been worth to be restored as an information center about the development and history of Scotch whisky. This whisky is only available to independent bottlers.

Dawson

This blend of the United Distillers group brings the memory of a Glasgow company, Peter Dawson Limited, which owned several distilleries, now totally disappeared, then used the Glen Ord brand after its absorption by the DCL group in 1925. It had a certain popularity in Scotland and it continues to have good sales in some export markets such as Canada, Chile and Norway.

Diner's

This range of standard and luxury blends is reserved for the network issuing the Diner's Club card, and is elaborated by the Red Lion Blending C°.

Doctor's Special

Created in the 20s by Robert McNish, this blend belonging to Allied Domecq is now distributed essentially in the Scandinavian countries where it is highly appreciated.

The Dominie

For the ancient Scots, this term inherited from Latin designated the Protestant pastor or the school teacher. Today it is the name of the rosette of a range of blends elaborated and distributed by the house Cockburn, founded in 1796 in Leith, near Edinburgh.

The Cockburn house is well known for its port, imported to England for more than a century. Their whiskies, likewise, enjoy an excellent reputation, and are cited in the inventory of the cellar of the writer Charles Dickens, established at his death in 1870. It also had among his clients no less than Sir Walter Scott, as well as numerous aristocrats and even some members of the British Royal Family.

For a time owned by the family that produced the Drambuie, Cockburn today belongs to a wine society, which intends to re-launch the range of blends and even propose a single malt with its name.

Edradour

Type: **single malt.**
Origin: **Highlands.**
Owner: **Campbell Distillers
(Pernod-Ricard).**
Date of birth: **1825.**

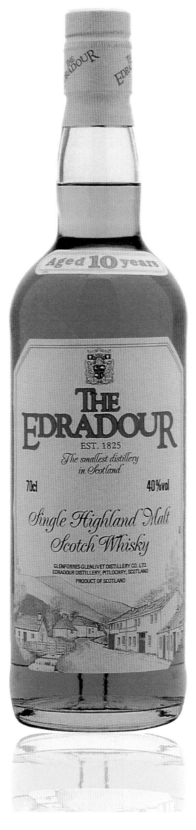

The smallest distillery in Scotland is also one of the oldest, since it was founded in 1825, and above all it is one of the best preserved since its origins. Indeed, it is one of the agricultural distilleries of the many that were in Scotland in that period.

The site is admirable: after several kilometers of winding road, the distillery is discovered as huddled in the hollow of a valley, along a stream of pure water that cascades over some black rocks. With its walls whitewashed with lime and its red doorways, the different buildings (malt, distillery, maturation cellars and storage sheds), offers a particularly picturesque set, already converted into a tourist attraction, near the town of Pitlochry.

Edradour owes its conservation to the intervention of a man, William Whiteley, called the «dean of distillers». Passionate about the qualities of this malt, he acquired the distillery in 1925, which allowed him to produce House of Lords, a luxury blend of great quality, and King Ransom's, which was once one of the most expensive whiskies in the world. Apart from the electrical installation in 1947 and the transformation of a barn into a reception room for visitors, nothing has changed in Edradour since its origin.

All operations are carried out manually by a team that does not exceed three people. Only the malting does not take place there. The stills are very small, their volume being the smallest authorized by the tax authorities. This legislation goes back to the era of smuggling, and was developed to prevent the multiplication of small-scale clandestine stills.

In such conditions, the production of Edradour is very limited, and in a year barely reaches the one made in a week by a classic Scottish distillery. After joining Campbell Distillers (Pernod Ricard) in 1982, Edradour began marketing its ten-year-old malt from the end of the 80s. Of superb aromatic complexity, it is not too powerful but it delights with its enormous harmony.

The Famous Grouse

Type: **blend.**
Origin: **Perth.**
Owner: **Matthew Gloag&Son.**
Date of birth: **1897.**

Before being the brand of a great Scottish blend, capercaillie was a symbol of the Highlands. This red grouse has these arid hills as its home. Their hunting demands a lot of talent and patience, to the point of being the national hunting of Scotland.

Thus, when Matthew Gloag decided to launch a blend in 1897, he named it «Grouse Brand», hoping to seduce the hunters of the Highlands, especially the gentlemen of the court. His daughter Philippa designed the label that represented the bird, although it was not colored until 1974.

Previously, the Cloag had distinguished themselves in the wine and liquor trade. The founder of the dynasty, Matthew Gloag, learned the trade in the famous Bordeaux wine business Calvet. It all started with the grocery and wine store, opened in 1800 in Perth, in the Highlands, by Matthew Gloag. His fame increased rapidly, to the point of becoming the exclusive supplier of the banquet given in 1842 in homage to Queen Vitoria, on the occasion of her first official trip to Scotland. His son William continued to develop the business, specializing in the importation of French wines. His nephew, also called Matthew, embarked in 1874 for Bordeaux, after seducing Octavio Calvet, the famous merchant, with his enthusiasm for trade. He returned to Perth twenty years later and, while continuing to be Calvet's official agent, decided to go into the whisky trade, which was very flourishing at the time. It is he who is responsible for the birth of the «Grouse Brand», which he soon transformed into «The Famous Grouse» brand.

The blend created by Matthew Gloag initially constituted only one activity among others, and it was not until the 1920s that it occupied the first place. This was primarily the work of Mathew's son, Matthew William, called «Willie», who conducted major advertising campaigns in Britain and then abroad. In 1917, the profits reached the record of 14.000 prompting society's accountants to «keep sales as low as possible», to escape as much as possible from the tax on the excessive benefits of wartime.

As the prohibition closed for some time the North American market, Willie Gloag knew how to avoid the difficulty developing in the neighboring countries, like the Antilles. And it was such an expansion that allowed Willie to have his own customs warehouse in 1936, accompanied by a very modern bottling chain for the time.

His son, Matthew Frederick, continued the development after the Second World War, especially with exports to the United States, Canada and Africa. And the dynasty continued in 1964 with the arrival of Matthew I Gloag. However, the family company joined the Highland Distilleries group in 1970, as the heirs could not face the very expensive inheritance rights. This did not prevent the promotion of the brand, one of the most consumed in Scotland and England.

The Famous Grouse has been described as an archetype of the true Scottish blend. Very aromatized, it is distinguished by a light peat perfume. It incorporates a significant percentage of single malts, especially since Highland Distilleries has some of the most famous: Tamdhu, Highland Park, Bunnahabhain, Glengassaugh, etc., offering a variety of aromatic characteristics that merge into The Famous Grouse, turning it into a true condensed scotch whisky. Once the blend is made, there is an additional aging of six months in order to harmonizes the set of different ingredients.

Apart from the standard, The Famous Grouse, it also exists in versions of twelve and twenty-one years of age.

AND ALSO...

Edward's

Recovering a blend (Sir Edward's) and a pure malt (Glen Edward's) this brand spread through the French market, being widespread by Bardinet group, number one of the rum, which also distributes the single malts Tamnavulin and Bowmore Legend. It is developed by Leith Distillers in Edinburgh.

Fettercairn

This distillery in the East of the Highlands began in 1824, but has undergone several transformations. Today it belongs to the Whyte&Mackay group, which markets a ten-year-old malt (previously eight years old), quite light and soft, with aromas of sherry.

Glen Deveron

Type: **single malt.**
Origin: **Highlands (Speyside).**
Owner: **William Lawson.**
Date of birth: **1962.**

Built in 1962, Macduff is one of the most recent distilleries in the Highlands. This small fishing port on the shores of the North Sea is at the mouth of Deveron, a river famous for its salmons. It gives the name to the single malt and not, a rare thing in Scotland, to the distillery itself.

A spring located in Banff, the neighboring town, ensures the supply of water. Its location near the sea and its position to the East take divisions among specialists: some classify the Macduff distillery in Speyside, while others reject such a thing.

In 1972, it was acquired by William Lawson, in order to ensure its supplies of malt. The blend, globally spread by the Martini&Rossi group (nowadays Bacardi-Martini), experienced good growth and its leaders wanted to reduce their dependence on external suppliers. The premises were enlarged and equipped with new facilities to treat the waste of the barley, after fermentation, which serve to feed the livestock. There is also a cooperage workshop for the repair of sherry casks that serve for aging.

If the essentials of Macduff's production are used for the elaboration of William Lawson's, the Glen Deveron, it is also commercialized in twelve years. Little peaty, it is characterized above all by its malted aromas, its roundness and its balanced softness. Often, it is presented as an excellent whisky to start, because it seduces much more than surprise. There are also whiskies with the name of Macduff and from this distillery that are older and distributed by independent bottlers.

Glendronach

Type: **single malt.**
Origin: **Highlands (Speyside).**
Owner: **Allied Distillers.**
Date of birth: **1826.**

With the name of a spring called Dronach, located near the town of Huntly, this distillery was built in 1826 on behalf of James Allardes. Quickly, its production was appreciated by the Duke of Gordon. Peer of the Realm, he was the one who imposed the law of 1823, taking the distillation of the underground, establishing the exploitation licenses and reducing taxation. But Allardes forgot to keep an eye on his distillery, which was partly destroyed by a fire in 1837.

A couplet of the turn of the century curiously mentions Glendronach, although perhaps it is only in favor of the rhyme:

«Cranberry ice-cream is good for the belly.

Ginger and walnuts are good for the intestine,

but Glendronach's wine is good for the stomach»

In 1960, Gledronach passed into the hands of Teacher. The group carried out important works that doubled its capacity, but fortunately without altering the authenticity of the place. Even traditional methods were preserved: malting in the square, with peat ovens and heated by charcoal stills.

Meanwhile, Glendronach proposed a very interesting choice for whisky tasters, as the twelve-year-old was proposed in two versions: «Original» aged in oak casks after containing whisky, and another aged in casks of sherry. With this it is possible to make subtle comparisons about the effects of these different types of casks, being the liquor identical at the beginning. Judging, however that the impregnation of sherry was too strong, the distillery suspended this double production several years ago and now only proposes a version called «Traditional», which unites the two previous malts. There is also an eighteen-year-old version.

Glenfarclas

Type: **single malt.**
Origin: **Highlands (Speyside).**
Owner: **J. and G. Grant.**
Date of birth: **1836.**

Originally a simple distillery installed in a Speyside farm, Glenfarclas passed into the hands of John Grant, a farmer of the region, in 1865. He developed well the production and soon his malts were famous for their excellent quality.

Very rare case in Scotland, the distillery remained in the hands of the same family, very independent, although the surname Grant is very popular in the country, especially in the world of whisky. George S. Grant, the current president, and his son John L.S. Grant, today represent the fourth and fifth generation. Extracting the water from a spring of melting snow, the Glenfarclas distillery has been modernized regularly, with stills that are among the largest in the region, and other improvements. It was also one of the first to offer a reception center for visitors, with a show and a tasting room. The Grant also breed Angus oxen, very famous. The great specificity of Glenfarclas is the aging of malts in sherry casks. A choice that involves many variations: some casks have contained only sherry, others have already been reused, and others have been used for an intermediate time for the passage of a whisky. Apart from the general quality of its production, widely spread throughout the world today, Glenfarclas occupies a special place among fans because of the importance of the range that is bottled and marketed: ten years, twelve years, fifteen years, twenty-one years, twenty-five years, and up to thirty years of age. As a rarity, the «105» is an unreduced whisky, of 60° whose age is not indicated (certainly less than ten years), and which offers a surprising aromatic quality without suffering from the potency of alcohol.

A wide range is also a real pleasure for the taster, since it presents a range of comparisons without parallel on the effects of aging. Also, there is a blend from the same house, the Glen Dowan.

In 1912, a rival distiller from London also praised the whiskies of Glenfarclas: «In that whisky one finds the sun and the shadow chasing each other over the fields of undulating wheat, the buzzing of the bee, the blowing of the month of May, the singing of the lark, the purple of the heather rising from the mist of the mountains, the morning dew and all the autumnal splendor that a captivating luminosity enriches with a golden explosion...» Particularly significative!

Glenfiddich

Type: **single malt.**
Origin: **Highlands (Speyside).**
Owner: **William Grant & Sons.**
Date of birth: **1886.**

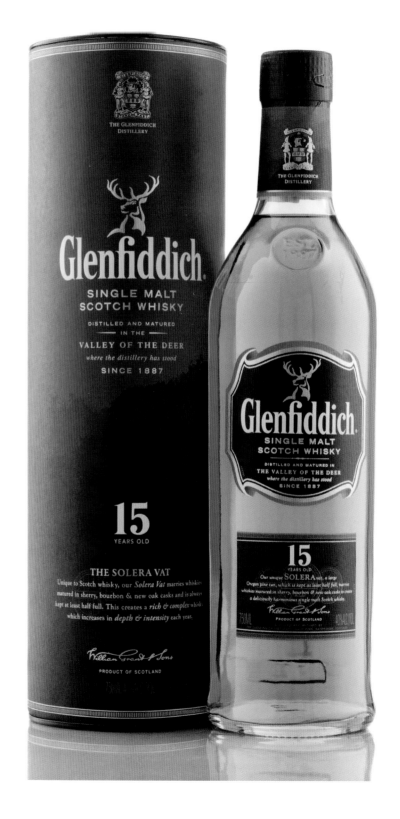

Just as Chivas Regal let the world know that there were other whiskies in addition to standard blends, Glenfiddich can vindicate the fact of having universally made known the existence of «single malts». This authentic commercial bet launched in 1963, first provoked a total disbelief in the whole of the profession, which believed that consumers would never accept the power and originality of the «malts».

Glenfiddich was rewarded for its pioneering determination with a first place ever contested since the brand represents a third of the sales of the whiskies.

Glenfiddich's bet is representative of the decision of the family of William Grant, the founder of the distillery in 1886. That son of a Dufftown tailor learned the arcana of making whisky in Morlach and saved for many years before being able to settle on his own. Thus he created his own distillery in a place called Glenfiddich (valley of the deer), fueled by the spring Robie Dubh, and acquired in Cardhu the stills and some material for a small sum. The first drop of whisky was distilled for the Christmas party of 1887. William Grant and then his family, owners of the business since its origin and always independent, began to be illustrated by the blend of their name, for which it was invented in 1957 a triangular bottle certainly original.

This was used for the Glenfiddich bottling in 1963, for the decision to market the «single malt». This conditioning should contribute to the success of the brand, especially with the export and in the «duty-free» shops. The Grant were the first to believe in the importance of this market, so they took care of the presentation of their whiskies by putting the bottles in cardboard boxes and in good quality metal boxes.

The expansion of Glenfiddich owes much to the commercial aggressiveness of society, but even more to the character of the malt. Clear and light, at least in its most widespread version, once eight years old and without date indication now, it is of great sweetness, along with a note of smoked and malted to differentiate itself from the blends. If the malting is not carried out today in the distillery, despite the presence of chimneys in the form of a pagoda, the stills, in various forms, are still heated directly to the coal. The bottling is done on site, a characteristic that Glenfiddich share only with Springbank.

Apart from the Special Reserve, the most widespread, there are other qualities of Glenfiddich whisky: eighteen, twenty-one and thirty years of age, plus some luxury versions in porcelain bottles, for the Far East. In 1991, nine fifty-year-old Glenfiddich boxes were sold at the London auctions at the price of $5.000 each. Glenfiddich was also the first distillery to open to visitors, with specific guides and a complete tour that allows to understand all the stages of the production of a whisky. Without being the oldest distillery of Dufftown, Glenfiddich is undoubtedly the one that incited others to settle and develop there.

Glengoyne

Type: **single malt.**
Origin: **Southern Highlands**
Owner: **Lang Brothers.**
Date of birth: **1833.**

Although located only about twenty kilometers from the center of Glasgow, the Glengoyne distillery benefits from a very pleasant country setting, not far from Lake Lomond. This landscape is certainly not uncommon to the large number of visitors that go there every year (more than 30.000). In addition, the distillery has keep its original architecture.

Founded in 1833 with the name of Glenguin, after Burnfoot of Dungoyne, it became property of Lang Brothers, in 1878, for the realization of the whiskies of that society of Glasgow. The line that separates the Highlands from the Lowlands passes close to these constructions, and this can be found in the characteristic style of the whiskies that are distilled there. In addition, there is a tradition in Glengoyme not to use peat at all stages of manufacturing, which gives pale and light whiskies, very close to those of the Lowlands.

But the selection of excellent barley and the aging of one third of the production in sherry casks provide great aromatic qualities to the Glengoyne whiskies, which are characterized by a great sweetness and softness, very pleasant. Today, two versions are mainly bottled, with a new packaging: ten years and seventeen years of age, the twelve years, very similar to ten years, is no longer marketed.

But Glengoyne also develops a very interesting vintage policy: the 1967 (marketed in 1992), the 1968 (marketed in 1993) or 1969 exactly distilled the day of the launch of Apollo I to the Moon (marketed in 1994). Each of these limited series (between 2.000 and 5.000 bottles) is subject to a precise description, often with a very little alcohol degree, 50,3° for example for 1968. These «occasion» bottles represent a commercial operation, but they are also of great interest for the expert.

A cask of Glengoyne, famous for its year.

Glen Grant

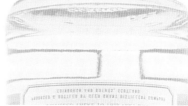

Type: **single malt.**
Origin: **Highlands (Speyside).**
Owner: **Seagram.**
Date of birth: **1839.**

Son of a farmer in the vicinity, the notary James Grant and his brother John created in 1839 a distillery in Rothes, next to the Spey. The two had some practice of whisky, first as clandestine distillers, then associated with the owners of Aberlour, and also knew about the grain trade. Passionate about modernism, James Grant had electricity installed in the distillery, which was one of the first in the Highlands to be so equipped. He played a major role in the construction of the Moray County Railroad, which allowed him to sell his whiskies beyond Rothes.

The activity of the distillery had a constant development, being directed later by the son of James, known as Major James Grant. The latter arranged the gardens of the distillery, famous today for their diversity and charm. He also arranged a small chest in the rock of a ravine through which a stream flows, in order to place a bottle of his whisky and some glasses, to offer them to his visitors, who were led to discover the place. The Major created in 1897 a second distillery in front of the first. But its partners in the operation failed and it was closed three years later to reopen in 1965, with the name of Caperdonich. The first achieved great prosperity and the Glen Grant whisky was one of the best known in Scotland at the beginning of the 20th century.

After a period of closure during the Second World War, Glen Grant merged in 1952 with The Glenlivet, and twenty years later with Longmorn. The group was finally acquired in 1978 by the Canadian group Seagram, owner of Chivas.

The production of Glen Grant is distinguished by the large number of different whiskies bottled: five years (sold in Italy), ten years, fifteen years, twenty-one years and twenty-five years of age. In addition, there are many older qualities (up to fifty years) and vintages among independent

Chest hidden in the gardens of Rothes. Major James Grant always kept a bottle for visitors.

bottlers. Several whiskies are clearly marked by the use of sherry casks for aging, but the most sold ones (especially the 40° one whose age has not been specified but which is undoubtedly between eight and ten years of age), are especially clear, of great finesse and beautiful balance. Seagram wanted to make the brand a leader for export, notably in new markets such as France.

The success of the five years of age in Italy is due to the efforts of a Milanese hotelier, Armando Giovanni, who, around 1950, left Scotland, where he had made a prospecting trip, with fifty boxes of Glen Grant, which he particularly appreciated. After making his countrymen love this whisky, he turned it into a real success, surpassing the sales of the Glen Grant half a million boxes.

The quality and variety of Glen Grant whiskies, especially the fifteen years and the twenty-one years of age, both sweet and dry with notes of sherry, grant them one of the best sales for export and an excellent reputation among the experts of well-balanced whiskies.

Glenkinchie

Type: **single malt.**
Origin: **Lowlands.**
Owner: **United Distillers.**
Date of birth: **1837.**

Although it is located only about twenty kilometers from Edinburgh, the Glenkinchie distillery is marked by rural origins that never really lost. There were two farmers, the Rate brothers, who founded it in 1837, in the town of Pencaitland. Here, they were able to perfectly use the barley they produced and malted themselves. The water, coming from the hills of Lammermuir, is of great sweetness, and the surroundings very pleasant. The name comes from a French family, the Quincy, installed in the region in the fourteenth century.

Although its malt quickly gained great renown, the Rate brothers bankrupt twenty years later, and the distillery almost disappeared, first transformed into a stable, then into a sawmill. But it was saved by its proximity to Edinburgh, and was acquired in the 1880s by a consortium of whisky dealers who needed it to make their blends.

The distillery was one of the fundamental pieces of the first regrouping of the distillers of the Lowlands, at the beginning of the century, under the name of «Scottish Malt Distillers», before joining the Haig group, then the DCL and finally the United Distillers. In this region of East Lothian, known as the «garden of Scotland», the raising of cattle has not lost its rights. Glenkinchie has owned his own farm for a long time, raising Angus oxen, who have won numerous awards in livestock contests. And the horses of Clydesdale, who strongly pulled the whisky carts through the streets of Glasgow, had a right every year to a well-deserved vacation in Glenkinchie.

Modernized after World War II, the distillery was arranged to receive visitors and the malting plant was transformed into a whisky museum. There is a model of a miniature distillery built in 1924 for the British Empire Exhibition. Reserved for blends for

long time, apart from a few vintages among independent bottlers, Glenkinchie's ten-year-old whisky came out of the shadows at the end of the 80s, thanks to its entry in the «Classic Malts» range. With a beautiful golden color, it is one of the most powerful whiskies of the Lowlands, with notes of peat and other floral, very characteristic. It offers a beautiful aromatic balance and a great sweetness.

The Glenlivet

Type: **single malt.**
Origin: **Highlands (Speyside).**
Owner: **Seagram.**
Date of birth: **1824.**

The River Livet only has a route of about thirty kilometers, before joining the Avon, and then the Spey, but its name is associated with Scotland's most elegant whisky: The Glenlivet. Its creator, George Smith, obtained his distiller's license in 1824, encouraged in this by the Duke of Gordon, lord of the region, who achieved the royal act that legalized the distillation, in 1823. But he had distilled clandestinely for some time in his farm, the same as his father, his grandfather and many of his neighbors.

His passage to legality was not, on the other hand, much appreciated, and the Lord of Aberlour offered him a pair of heavy pistols that he carried for several years, to discourage the resentment of his former clandestine companions. Smith was not really the family's real surname, since it previously was called «Gow», with much more Scottish resonances at a time when this made people suspect the desire for independence.

With the help of his son James Gordon, who joined him in 1850, George Smith changed places twice before settling definitively the distillery, in 1858, in the current site. The proximity of the railroad was decisive, but also a certain quality of water that passes long years by the mountains before flowing through multiple springs. Long before legalization, Glenlivet was already synonymous with great quality. Elizabeth Grant and Rothiemuceus thus described the flavor when he sent a bottle to King George IV in 1822: «[...] largely forest, sweet as milk, and with the true taste of contraband...»

When the whiskies began to be known outside the Highlands, be part of the region of the Livet was one of the first signs of distinction and quality, to the point that James Gordon Smith decided to officially

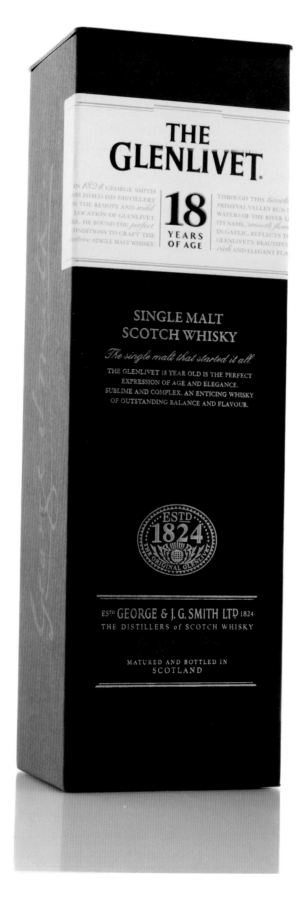

The Glenlivet distillery, modernized on numerous occasions, is not very typical.

Glenmorangie

Type: **single malt.**
Origin: **Northern Highlands.**
Owner: **Macdonald & Muir.**
Date of birth: **1843.**

The distillery was officially founded in Tain, in 1843, by William Matheson, but this whole region of the Northern Highlands practiced distillation many decades earlier. The buildings already housed a brewery, whose production had been famous since the Middle Ages.

Due to lack of resources, Matheson had to used second-hand stills, which were the largest in Scotland (5,14 m), although they had little capacity. However, the liquor produced had such a character that its successors always manufactured it identically.

These stills produced lighter but higher purity alcohols. For the rest, novelty for the time, they were heated to steam (and not directly to the flame), which contributed to the obtaining of a less aggressive liquor. Other distinctive factors: the water is clearly more mineralized than elsewhere in Scotland, from the spring of Tarlogie; a specific yeast for whisky; aging exclusively in casks of bourbon, less aggressive aromatically than sherry; a peat (used in small quantities) younger and more brittle than other whiskies.

All these specific conditions produce a whisky of great originality. Very round and floral, not very smoky, offers a good structure without aggression, with an amazing aromatic diversity: an expert perfumer would identify up to twenty-six different aromas, such as apricot, bergamot, cinnamon and quince.

This whisky was soon known throughout Scotland, particularly because the proximity of the railway allowed easy distribution. And expatriates from Ross County, where the small town of Tain is located, were also excellent propagandists.

Incorporated in 1887, the distillery was modernized several times, although without changing its original structures. Tra-

intervene in 1880. Thus he obtained legally that only his whisky could be called «The Glenlivet» while eighteen other distilleries could add the term «Glenlivet», to their names, but only in the second place, considering that these distilleries are quite far from the River Livet. Two of them have already closed.

Thanks to the efforts of Bill Smith Grant, grandson of James Gordon Smith, The Glenlivet knew an enormous fame in the North American market, long before the time of the prohibition. After its merger with Glen Grant, the distillery was modernized several times, as well as the brand, they entered the Seagram group in 1978. The commercial strength of this group made Glenlivet one of the most wide-

spread whiskies and, above all, of the most renowned in the world. Few things in its development distinguish The Glenlivet twelve years old from other Speyside whiskies, but it has a unique character, easily recognizable in a blind tasting. A great elegance, a perfect balance between malted and fruity aromas, a long duration in the mouth justify its place as leader and symbol of the Speyside style. Aging is made by a third in the casks that have contained sherry.

Apart from the twelve years, the distillery bottled an eighteen year and a twenty-one-year-old, the latter more marked because its sherry aromas And independent bottlers have many varieties, sometimes vintage, or not reduced. The label «George&J. G. Smith's Glenlivet Whisky».

dition states that sixteen different artisans (the brewer, the distiller, the boilermaker, the cooper, etc.) ensured production from its origins, each transmitting to his successor his skill and manufacturing secrets. In 1918, after two years of closure by the war, the need for capital led to the sale of the business to its main client, the blender of Leith Macdonald&Muir. Well exported to the United States, the production of Glenmorangie suffered from prohibition, then the recession of 1929, and the distillery was closed from 1931 to 1936.

It was necessary to wait the end of the Second World War for prosperity to return. Since then, the production has not stopped developing, passing the stills to four units in 1980 and eight in 1990.

Glen Moray

Type: **single malt.**
Origin: **Highlands (Speyside).**
Owner: **Macdonald & Muir.**
Date of birth: **1897.**

Apart from a certain phonetic similarity, Glen Moray has some common points with Glenmorangie, starting with the same owner, Macdonald&Muir and having been both breweries before being distilleries.

The creation of Glen Moray in 1897 is due to both to the abundance and the quality of the waters in the area, as well as the proximity of the city of Elgin. Former episcopal seat and capital of the north of Scotland, this city was in the last century an important center for the whisky business, and one of the main independent bottlers, Gordon & MacPhail, still has its warehouse and storages here. In addition, the entire Moray region is renowned for the quality of its malt barley: according to a local axiom, during the summer the sun shines there forty days more than in any other part of Scotland.

After its acquisition by MacDonald&Muir in 1920, Glen Moray consecrated the essence of its production to the preparation of blends and was considerably enlarged in 1958.

However, the whisky is proud of its «Glenlivet» suffix and, more recently, the commercialization of the different varieties has been undertaken on a large scale. Although pale in color, quite light and of good elegance, it is a round and soft whisky. The twelve years of age is the most common variety, but there is also a fifteen-year-old, a seventeen-year-old and a few vintages: 1973,1966, 1964 and 1962, especially. The bottle, exclusive model of the brand, reproduces the shape of a traditional still, and Glen Moray is also available in metal boxes decorated with the different uniforms of the Highland regiments, very appreciated by collectors.

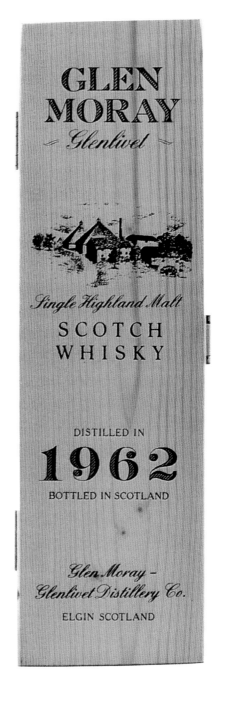

Glen Ord

Type: **single malt.**
Origin: **Northern Highlands.**
Owner: **United Distillers.**
Date of birth: **1838.**

Located near Black Island, a greener region than its name suggests, this distillery was created in 1838, in the town of Muir of Ord. The region was once famous for its clandestine distillers, but it was in an old flour mill where Robert Johnstone and Donald McLennan settled. They benefited from the generosity of the lord of the region, Thomas MacKenzie, who granted them the distillery without paying rent, preferring that this activity be developed to better remunerate the farmers of that lands and create new jobs. The MacKenzie from Ord also had the privilege of grinding barley and oats since the early seventeenth century. The distillery also benefited from the same water coming from the White Burn spring and used by the flour mill. And the proximity of Inverness, some twenty kilometers away, also favored commercial development. Apart from having its own malting, the distillery had the peculiarity of adding heather to the peat in the malting, which provided much drier aromas.

Acquired in 1920 by Dewar, the distillery has provided malts for the elaboration of Dewar's blend. But the commercialization of «single malt» has been curiously hampered by the multiplication of its names. Not only was the distillery called Muir of Ord, Glen Ord and Ord, but the label of its bottles also bore the mention of Glenordie, which really discouraged its consumers, even the most addicted.

The good order was arranged by United Distillers with the unique name of «Glen Ord», both for the distillery and for the brand. The commercialized version is twelve years old, powerful and soft at the same time, with a beautiful amber color and a perfect roundness. There is still a twelve-year-old Glenordie and a twenty-four-year Ord.

Glenturret

Type: **single malt.**
Origin: **Highlands.**
Owner: **Highland Distilleries.**
Date of birth: **1775.**

Proclaimed the oldest distillery in Scotland, Glenturret has buildings dating back to 1775, and some elements testify the presence in the area of distillers since 1717. It was clandestine and the place suited it, because, although being close to Crieff, the distillery was, in fact, in a deep valley, surrounded by wooded mountains. His discretion of yesteryear gives it a very picturesque charm in every season, today. The whole region is very touristy, especially for golf and fishing.

From Lake Turret and fed by the melting snow, this water of great purity falls into the river of the same name that runs at the foot of the distillery.

This remarkable antiquity and place did not prevent the distillery from being completely shut down in 1920. It took all the energy and passion of one man, James Fairlie, to resuscitate it in 1957. Taking advantage of the old buildings, he looked for artisanal traditions in the processing of his malts. But he also made of Glenturret an important tourist center, which in 1994 received more than 200,000 visitors. Not only can you make a complete visit to the distillery, with audiovisual projection and tasting of the products of the distillery, but there is a good restaurant under the «pagoda» of the old malt house. There is a bagpiper that welcome the groups, and the menus are part of the purest Scottish cuisine.

The Glenturret whiskies also deserve a «visit», as evidenced by the numerous rewards they have received since the rebirth of the distillery. Of rather pale color, they are quite malted, with special floral aromas. The older ones have very strong scent of sherry.

The eight and the twelve years of age are the most common, but there is a ten year not rectified (only available in the distillery), a fifteen-year-old and some limited editions like the «5.000 days», and the vintages of 1972, 1967 and 1966.

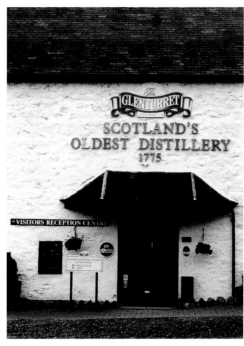

Taken at the dawn of 1900, this panoramic view of the distillery is a photomontage, since the wide-angle lens had not been invented yet. Well preserved, Glenturret is nowadays one of the most picturesque distilleries in Scotland.

In twenty-four years of good and legal services, Towsen the cat has caught at least 28,899 mice in the Glenturret barns. It should appear in the Guinness Book of Records.

Grant's

Type: **blend.**
Origin: **Glasgow.**
Owner: **William Grant&Sons.**
Date of birth: **1898.**

The birth of this blend, one of the best known in the world, which also knows a great growth today, is born out to one of the most famous failures of the whisky business.

In 1886, after several years of saving, William Grant built his distilleries, Glenfiddich, and then Balvenie.

Its main customer was Pattison Limited, a blending merchant of the time. In a completely unexpected way, he went bankrupt in 1898, endangering the activity of William Grant and his seven children.

Bravely, they decided to embark on the elaboration and commercialization of their own blend, choosing as their brand the currency of their clan, «Stand fast». A son-in-law, Charles Gordon, was commissioned to open a store in Glasgow, in an abandoned church, and to market the brand.

William Grant and his wife Elizabeth.

A delivery truck from the 1920s in the Philippines: export has always been an important point in the development of Grant's.

The beginnings were difficult. In 503 sales visits he managed to sell a box of twelve bottles only. But Charles Gordon did not get discouraged and continued with his efforts in Scotland, and then throughout Britain. At the same time, other members of the family try the export and, before the First World War, the society had sixty agencies in thirty different countries.

William Grant (who died in 1923), his sons and then his grandsons, managed to survive the different crises of both wars, the prohibition and the Great Depression. Particularly in this period, of the six still active distilleries, two belonged to the Grant family.

In addition, Grant was able to continue to be completely independent and family-owned until today. It is chaired by a member of the fourth generation, Sandy Grant Gordon, and nine direct descendants of the founder occupy the directorial functions in society. After the Second World War it distinguished itself from the competitors, it was revived and adopted for its blend a triangular bottle, very rare. His success was such that it was adopted

immediately for the Glenfiddich whisky. To respond to the demand, the group has opened a grain distillery in Girvan, and two more in Malta, also in Girvan and in Kininvie.

A frame from the film *Whisky a gogo*.

AND ALSO...

Gairloch

This blend created in 1904 by McMullen&Sons, has the distinctive characteristic of being made with magnificent malts, such as Glengoyne, Glen Rothes, Highland Park, Tamdhu and Macallan, combined at the age of three or four years.

Glen Blair

This «pure malt» (blend of different singles malts) is a twelve-year-old marketed by Burn Stewart.

Glen Drumm

Marketed by Douglas Laing of Glasgow, this «pure malt» is mixed in the Longside distillery. Conceived as an introduction to the universe of whiskies, it is presented in bottles numbered for their authenticity.

Glendullan

This Speyside distillery, in Dufftown, the latest of the seven installed in the whisky capital, has always served to refill the blenders, whether William Williams, its founders, or United Distillers, the current owner, mainly for the brand Old Parr.

However, it exists in small quantities in bottles, especially in the «Flora and Fauna» series, and among the independents.

Glen Elgin

This representative Speyside Malt is used in the production of Whisky Horse, but it is also bottled in small quantities of twelve years of age.

Glenesk

Founded in 1898 from some linen spinning, this distillery from the East of the Highlands has had a very busy existence,

alternating closures and modifications, in malting then in grain distillery. Its rather light malt serves primarily for the elaboration of Vat 69 although it is also sometimes bottled.

Glen Garioch

This distillery in the Aberdeen region dates back to 1798 and belonged to William Sanderson (Vat. 69) and later to DCL, before joining the Morrison-Bowmore group. It has the peculiarity of reuse the heat of the distillation to warm greenhouses of tomatoes and green vegetables.

Glen Garioch malt (pronounced «Glen Guerie»), used mainly for the production of the Rob Roy blend, is bottled in small quantities and is appreciated for its peat aromas.

Glen Keith

Although built in an old flour mill with materials from the region, this modern distillery (built in Speyside in 1957) uses some cutting-edge techniques, such as the heating of stills with gas and the computerization of production. Used primarily for the production of Chivas Regal, this liquor begins to be bottled at ten years of age.

Glen Lossie

With the name of a Speyside river, this distillery dates from 1876, but was modernized twenty years later, and even more after World War II. Used mainly for the production of Haig blends, it is bottled at ten years of age in the series «Flora and Fauna».

Glen Roger's

This eight-year-old «single malt» is bottled, without indication of the distillery of origin, for the William Pitters group, mainly destined to the French market.

Glen Rothes

This distillery of Speyside, which has the right of the «Glenlivet» indication, produces a malt so appreciated by the blenders (notably by The Famous Grouse), that it is difficult to find it in bottles, apart from Berry Bros&Rudd (for twelve years and fifteen years of age) and among the independents.

Glen Scotia

With Springbank, it is one of two distilleries active in Campbeltown, which had more than thirty. Despite major modernization in the late 1970s, it closed in 1984, before being acquired five years later by the Canadian Gibson group. There are still excellent malts of the period before the

closing, waiting for the current production to have age a lot.

Glen Turner

Essentially distributed in France by the La Martiniquaise group, this pure eight-year-old whisky has conquered one of the first places in the whisky market.

Grand Macnish

Created in 1863 in Glasgow, this blend was conceived as lighter than the others, with a strong aromatic personality. More than forty different whiskies come into its composition. The brand has changed owners several times, especially the Canadian Industrial Alcohol group, before falling into the orbit of Hiram Walker, and finally ending up as the property of the MacDuff group in 1991.

Haig

Type: **blend.**
Origin: **Markinch.**
Owner: **United Distillers.**
Date of birth: **1850.**

There are not many families as intimately linked to the history of whisky and Scotland as the Haig. Arrived with William the Conqueror, the Haig, that were called Hage, settled in the XIII century on the banks of the Tweed. First they were warriors, showing off in the Crusades, as well as in the First World War. Robert Haig was one of the first clandestine distillers known: in 1655, that farmer from Throsk was warned by the parish council to have distilled Easter Saturday

The first known John Haig, a descendant of Robert, married Margaret Stein in 1751, whose family owned several distilleries. His five children continued the family tradition in the Edinburgh region, and also in Dublin. The original distillery, in Kilbagie, was at the end of the 18th century one of the most important in Scotland, supplying mainly the London producers in Geneva.

John Haig, who gave his name to the current blend, also creates the Cameronbridge distillery, which he transformed into a grain distillery thanks to the invention of his cousin Robert Stein, the continuous still. Always looking for perfection, he replaced it in 1831 with the Cooffey still, more effective for distillation in large quantities. It was around 1850 when the Haig blend appeared, which quickly gained great popularity. John Haig has not been satisfied with just the development of the production tool, but was interested in advertising, making a white schooner sail on the beaches of the English Channel with the slogan: «Do you know John Haig?». He was also one of the artisans of the first group of cereal distillers that in 1877 gave birth to the DCL group, being one of its first directors, along with his son. Upon his death in 1878, his society produced more than 5.5 million liters of whisky. His youngest son, Douglas Haig, has distinguished himself during the First World War. Commander-in-chief of the British forces in France, he was named Earl of Haig, and after the war resumed the direction of his company.

Since a new blending unit was created in Markinch, the brand has continued to progress to the point of being the most sold in the UK, just before the Second World War. In the 20s, his slogan «Do not be lazy, ask for a Haig» have very success. Of amber color and powerful for being a blend, the Haig is a traditionally brand of excellent quality. In 1986, after some antitrust restrictions, its commercialization in Great Britain was entrusted to Whyte&Mackay, but the export belongs to United Distillers.

Highland Park

Type: **single malt.**
Origin: **Orkney Islands**
Owner: **Highland Distilleries.**
Date of birth: **1798.**

The beginnings of distillation in the Orkney Islands probably date back to the mid-eighteenth century and are marked by clandestinely and contraband. However, even the notables of the town had a double game, like William Traill, son of smugglers, who established an official distillery and brewery in the early nineteenth century, but used the underground to sell his whisky.

One of them, Magnus Eunson, who founded a distillery where Highland Park is now located in Kirkwall, had as an accomplice one of his relatives who acquired his whisky in the local church. When Robert Borwick officially created the Highland Park distillery in 1822, he called John Robertson to direct it, who was none other than the officer who had arrested Magnus Eunson ten years earlier for illegal distillation.

The Orkney Archipelago has some sixty islands, half of them uninhabitable. The largest houses Kirkwall, and the site of Highland Park was considered because of the quality of the waters of two powerful neighboring springs, but also because of the proximity of the sea to the expeditions.

A famous episode took place in 1883: on the occasion of the inauguration of the Union Castle shipping line, the Highland

It is not only the northernmost distillery in Scotland, but also in the whole world!

Park whisky was so much appreciated on board that it was served, once get to Copenhagen, to the Tsar of Russia and numerous personalities who were delighted of it.

The distillery became property of James Grant in 1908, and then, in 1937, of the group Highland Distilleries. Towards the 70s this whisky was commercialized by itself, since the blenders had long been appreciating the qualities that catalyzed the characteristics of the other malts. Apart from its mineralized water, Highland Park is distinguished by the use of a very aromatic peat, with marine scents. The barley is grown right there and, on the occasion of the malting, a little heather is added to the peat.

All these conditions make Highland Park a particularly appreciated malt. For Michael Jackson, one of the authorities of whisky, it brings together «all the virtues that can be expected from malts», smoked, peaty, malting, sherry notes, soft, mellow, all in one great aromatic harmony, with a beautiful duration. This enthusiasm was confirmed during the great tasting carried out in 1984 by the newspaper «The Scotsman», where the Highland Park was the only whisky that achieved a hundred percent. Twelve years of age is the most common quality, although there is also the eight years one. There are also some vintages, like 1967, bottled after twenty-four years of maturation, and that some tasters describe as «mystic».

House of Lords

Type: **blend.**
Origin: **Pitlochry.**
Owner: **Campbell Distillers.**
Date of birth: **1925.**

This luxury blend owes everything to the passion of William Whiteley, nicknamed «the dean of the distillers». Passionate about malts, he buys in 1925 the Edradour distillery, the smallest in Scotland, of which he particularly appreciates the qualities. But at the time the «single malt», was not yet fashionable, and he devotes a part of the production to the elaboration of a blend of a high range, which he baptizes with the name of the House of Lords.

Nowadays, this blend is available in the United Kingdom, in Parliament, in Westminster. It is even exported to a hundred countries. To authenticate this brand, Whiteley has managed to add to his heraldry the griffons (fabulous animals) identical to those of Westminster. William Whiteley is concerned about achieving perfection in the development of his blends that he even travels in a limousine, in order not to spoil his smell by breathing the smoke of the trains of the time. And he did not turn off his thirst even with the soda of the Highlands!

To ensure a better aging of its blends, Whiteley also thinks of making them travel for a year by sea, to make sure the rocking of the ship can favor the perfect harmonization of the different components. The House of Lords knew a remarkable success during the American prohibition, especially in the clandestine bars. Metallic containers were manufactured especially for dispatch: they were loose in the vicinity of the American coasts before being recovered by the retailers. There were also clandestine carriers from Canada, including submarines that reached the foot of the New York skyscrapers. These scenarios worthy of the series «The Incorruptible» are confirmed by many official reports, such as the story of the Long Island embargo of the British ship *Rosie M.B.* that contained House of

Lords for a value of 300,000 dollars, load distributed in a series of metallic torpedoes each one of which contained around 150 liters. Very soft, particularly charming and full-bodied, House of Lords is now available in two qualities, eight years old and twelve years old.

AND ALSO...

Hankey Bannister

This brand of blends (standard and eight, twelve, fifteen and twenty years) today is distributed by Inver House and is named after a wine and spirits business in the elegant West End neighborhood of London, which existed after 1757 and had as its clientele the majority of the aristocratic society. The brand was proposed from 1890. Re-acquired by another company in 1932, Hankey Bannister was introduced into military centers, then into diplomatic circles. The brand continues to progress today, especially in the field of export.

Hedges & Butler Royal

This wine business partnership dates back to 1667 and benefits from the support of the royal household after Charles II. It has eleven titles of monarchy suppliers throughout Europe to Japan. His blends (standard and twelve years) date from between the two World Wars, and was reacquired by the Bass brewery.

Highland Blend

The Avery's wine business was established in Bristol in the 18th century. The group of wines is always its main activity, but created this brand of blend, which was baptized as Queen Elizabeth, with some success, even when it was no longer manufactured.

Highland Queen

This luxury blend (fifteen and twenty-one years old) has been produced in homage to Marie Stuart, Queen of Scotland, by MacDonald&Muir, blender of Leith, near Edinburgh, after 1893. The brand was heavily exported.

House of Peers

Created in 1947 by Douglas Laing, blender of Glasgow, this range of blends is called « House of Peers », another name of the House of Lords. It is packed in a small chubby bottle, traditionally nicknamed «maillet de macón». There are different qualities: Luxury, XO Extra Old, twelve and twenty-two years. Douglas Laing's ability is to choose very young grain whiskies and associate them with old malts from all over Scotland. It comes in this way to propose blends of high quality, particularly soft and aromatic, with reasonable prices.

100 (Hundred) Pipers

Created by the Seagram group in 1965, this brand of blend goes on the market with competitive prices, thus containing quality whisky, like those of The Glenlivet or Glen Gran. It experiences a great growth, especially in the Hispanic world.

Invergordon

Type: **single malt.**
Origin: **Northern Highlands.**
Owner: **Invergordon.**
Date of birth: **1960.**

The only Highland grain distillery (except Lomond, located two steps from the Lowlands) is located to the north, on the estuary of Cromarty. Its situation is explained by the quality and abundance of cereals in the region, but it was also due to the closure of a naval base of the Royal Navy. Invergordon is in effect a port in deep water that was long used by the admiralty. To compensate for the loss of jobs by the removal of the base, the distillery was built in 1960. It is a modern facility, which expanded in 1988. Its production quickly became important, reaching 40 million liters of grain whisky, and also produces neutral alcohol for gin and vodka. The essence of the production of whisky is devoted to the blends, but the company is also specializing in the commercialization of numerous brands to the different foreign markets. Elsewhere, it creates the Whyte&Mackay group (with the giant American Brands), which ensures numerous outlets for its different whiskies.

In 1990, Invergordon began to market its grain whisky under its own brand and, with the difference of United Distillers with Cameron Brig, it tries to spread beyond Scotland, targeting non-whisky consumers. Some malted barley does not enter the distillation process. It is a ten-year-old (there is another version, with no predicted age), very pale and pure in flavor, quite floral with aromas. With the risk of dissatisfy purists, and in any case modifying customs, it is better appreciated with ice cubes than in its pure state or with cold water.

Inver House

Type: **blend.**
Origin: **Airdrie.**
Owner: **Inver House.**
Date of birth: 1965.

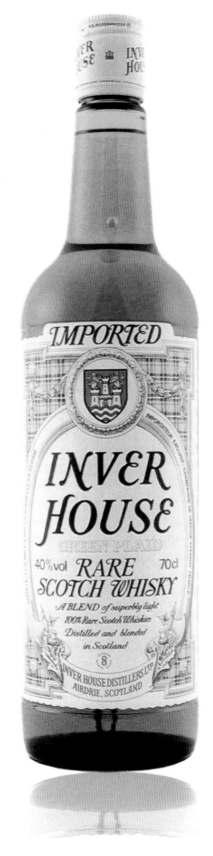

Founded in 1965 in Airdrie, near Glasgow, by the American group Publicker, the company has taken a different direction in 1988, when it was repurchased by its superiors: William Robison, Graeme Thomson, Angus Graham and Bob Boyle.

It became completely independent and what is more, Scottish. The strategy of the new leaders was to develop blends for export and to acquire malt distilleries.

Inver House had many other blends with another brand of blend, also called Green Plaid, (like Catto's, one of the first brand blends in history), in this way different whiskies are born from the distilleries that belong to it: Speyburn, Knockdhu and Pulteney. The particularity of the group is the importance of its exports: 95% of the volume traded in seventy-five countries. At this point many of their brands are absent in the British market. This success earned it «The Queen's Award for Export Achievement», in 1982, an official reward for the importance of the volumes exported. The blend belongs to the category of light whiskies, also with good color and strength, which know a great export boom after many years. It is appreciated not only, but especially, in long drink. There are more rare versions: the twelve years, the twenty-one years and the thirty-five years of age, the latter presented in a glass carafe with a pond base.

J & B

Type: **blend.**
Origin: **Strathleven (Glasgow).**
Owner: **IDV (Grand Metropolitan).**
Date of birth: **1831.**

The second most sold whisky in the world come from... a love story! The Bolognese Giacomo Justerini (the «J» of J&B) arrives in London in 1749 following an opera singer, from his native Italy. History has left us nothing written, unfortunately, about what happened with this relationship. What is certain, is that the young Justerini established himself the same year in the British capital, associating with an Englishman, George Johnson, to create a store of wines and spirits. The business quickly has a great success, since, eleven years later, they receive a patent from the supplier of the royal crown, the first of a long series.

In 1831, the business was retaken by Alfred Brooks (the «B» of the logo), which retains the name of Justerini in his signature.

Whisky comes to a preponderant activity of society, which launches its first blend, bearing the Club brand, around 1880. It is only sold in stores in London and Edinburgh. At the time, Justerini&Brooks owned one of the most important stocks of old Scotch whiskies.

The true beginning of the J&B blend dates from the end of the American prohibition in 1933, when this clear whisky becomes fashionable in New York. But it will be necessary to wait until the 1950s for its spread throughout the United States, then in Europe. The J&B Rare is indeed a new fad of whisky, that of pale blends which find their place in nightclubs and bars. Consumed with ice or long drink, they seduce a great clientele for their naturalness and smoothness, leading J&B to the second world brand.

For this reason, the St. James' Street London warehouse became a great compa-

J&B, the magical initials, well exploited by advertising and sponsoring.

John Player Special

Type: **blend.**
Origin: **Glasgow.**
Owner: **Douglas Laing.**
Date of birth: **1960 approx.**

ny. In the 1950s, it became United Wines Traders, then, ten years later, it merged with the Gilbey gin house to become IDV (International Distillers and Vintners). In 1972, the group is bought by a giant of hospitality industry, Grand Metropolitan. On the other hand, it had become the owner of four whisky distilleries (Knockando, Auchroisk, Strathmill and Glen Spey, all located in Speyside).

If you wanted a true quintessence of Scotch whisky, the J&B Rare did not hesitate to discover its origins, an unusual attitude for a blend. At least forty-two different whiskies come into its composition, covering all of the different production regions: grain whiskies, Lowlands, Highlands, Speyside, Campbeltown and Islay malts. Even the distilleries, always the most prestigious, are known: some of these from the group, The Glenlivet, Glen Grant, Macallan, Longmorn, Glenfiddich contribute to the final blend. Only the exact proportions of the final blend are missing... All these malts are at least five years old, and often eight and more. On the other hand, the different Speyside malts undergo a common supplementary aging one year before the final blend,

which spend a few months in casks, being bottled. Another particularity of J&B: the refusal to make it mature, and the absence of candy, explains its pale color. Fresh and fruity, with a lot of softness and a slight smoky point, the J&B is ready to conquer the world. If the Rare *(sic...)* evidently constitutes the essential part of J&B's sales, the family was enlarged: the reserve is fifteen years, much longer in the mouth and more amber in color; more recently they have launched J&B Jet, a twelve-year-old, in which the malts come only from Speyside, and which benefits from a cutting-edge presentation: opaque black bottle, gold letters and red cap.

In the last century, the British John Player has achieved his reputation for his knowledge of tobacco and his ability to mix different crops and obtain high quality cigarettes. The John Player Special brand, which currently belongs to the British American Tobacco group, has an international standing, especially in the export and duty-free stores.

A rare occurrence in the universe of whiskies, JPS also became a brand of quality blends, which reproduces the logo of cigarettes and their characteristic black color. Its «elitist» position is similar and ensures its best outlets in the Far East and the entire Pacific area. Developed by Douglas Laing, the range comprises three qualities: the Fine Old, quite strong in flavor; the twelve years, made with malts from different regions of Scotland; the Rare (or Special Rare), in which there are at least twenty-five different malts, -some with certain age, twenty-five years, with the presence of turkey malts from Islay- and with each bottle numbered.

Douglas Laing has created his company in Glasgow in 1950, which has become familiar and independent. It is currently run by his sons Fred and Stewart. They have constituted a stock with very old malts that they use to improve their blends and to elaborate in this way luxury whiskies, very soft and to savor a long time in the mouth. Its main markets are export, especially in the Far East and the Pacific area.

Johnnie Walker

Type: **blend.**
Origin: **Kilmarnock.**
Owner: **United Distillers.**
Date of birth: **1909.**

Johnnie Walker's blending room at the beginning of the 20th century.

The world number one of the whisky brands is named after a son of the Scottish farmer from Ayrshire, south of Glasgow. In 1820, John Alexander Walker was installed as a shopkeeper in the small town of Kilmarnock. He sold everything, but also whisky, and especially a blend, called «Walkers Kilmarnock Whisky», which dates back to 1850. The construction of the London-Glasgow railway line, which passes through Kilmarnock, helps him develop his sales outside of its origin region. A flood causes the entire stock they had in the store to be destroyed in 1852, so John Walker, helped by his son Alexander, becomes only a wholesaler of whiskies.

The development continued quickly, the Walkers especially use a distribution system by the merchant marine: the captains leave Glasgow carrying with them boxes of whiskies that they sell in their different scales all over the world, taking advantage of the trip. Became the patron of the business in 1865, Alexander Walker created especially the blend brand Johnnie Walker's Old Highland Whisky. The original recipe is kept in the archives of the society, and recently recreated, this blend was particularly

strong, with very marked peat aromas, and quite different from a modern whisky. On the other hand, Alexander Walker opens some offices in London, then in Birmingham and Manchester, and also in Australia. When he died in 1890, his society was already one of the most important in the Scotch whisky market.

His sons, George Patterson and Alexander, continue with the development, and in 1893 they acquired the Cardhu distillery, after long negotiations with its owner, Elizabeth Cumming. Their malts were already one of the bases of the blends of the Walker house, and that's why they made the purchase to ensure the exclusivity.

The Walker brothers, soon reinforced by Elizabeth Cumming's son, John Fleetwood, develop their blends throughout the world, especially the Very Special Old Highland and the Extra Special. But, at the beginning of the century, the Walkers realize that the demand of consumers evolves and that it is necessary to adapt their products to it.

This will be especially the work of its director, James Stevenson. At this point they introduce two blends, one standard and a softer and sweeter luxury. In the search for

JOHNNIE WALKER®

Red Label®

Blended Scotch Whisky

DISTILLED, BLENDED AND BOTTLED IN SCOTLAND

an advertising, they call the designer Tom Browne. In memory of the founder of the society, he creates a dandy character, with a hat, glasses and a walking stick, walking completely straight. An attitude confirmed by the slogan «Born in 1820... and always reinforcing itself».

The success is such that the two blends take the names of Johnnie Walker Red Label for the standard, Johnnie Walker Black Label for twelve years. Stevenson also made the choice of the square bottle and the in-

George Patterson Walker was president of Johnnie Walker for twenty-five years.

clined label. His success will not be denied, as his recipes are not changed until today. It is in 1925 when Johnnie Walker meets the group DCL (today United Distillers), where he becomes the mainstay of society. But the world number one of the Scottish blend will never leave the town of its founder, and it is still in Kilmarnock, near the station, where the bottling factory is located, with a production capacity of 2 million bottles per week.

Parallel to the evolution of the sales of whiskies, the dandy Johnnie Walker became a true star of advertising, first in ads, then in the form of statuettes of all sizes, which have become real collectibles. Specialists can even find the date of manufacture based on the color of the boots or the shape of the cane from which the dandy never separates. In the 50s, it takes human form for promotional tours in bars and cafes. In France, this advertising campaign was introduced the first time by the company Simón Fréres, distributors of the brand at that time.

Old bottles of Johnnie Walker and its original delivery box in wood.

Jura

Type: **single malt.**
Origin: **Jura.**
Owner: **Invergordon.**
Date of birth: **1810.**

More than forty different whiskies are involved in the development of the Red Label. As for the Black Label, it only carries malts of at least twelve years, with the significant presence of Cardhu malts but also of Taliske.

The Johnnie Walker range is not limited to its two stellar brands, each one a world leader in its category; The Black Label was rated one of the ten best-selling blenders in the world. It also includes more confidential varieties, often reserved for export and markets such as duty-free stores: the Blue Label, each copy numbered; the Gold Label, eighteen years old; the Premier, presented in a bottle very different from the classic version; The Swing (which exists in two versions, standard and luxury), where the originality is in the bottle, conceived for recreational boaters, round and squat, that oscillates on itself but never reverses... Which makes it resist all the roll and nod of the seas of the world, without ever losing the minimum taste of this precious liquid.

The island of Jura is close to that of Islay, but they differ in numerous points. Very mountainous, dominated by two twin mountains called *paps,* a term that also designates a female chest in Scotland. Rather austere, the island is not too populated: less than 200 inhabitants. The name of the island comes from a word that means «fallow deer», an etymology entirely justified by the presence of many thousands of these cervids in the forest that covers a large part of the island. Apart from its only distillery, Jura is equally known for the passage that George Orwell wrote, in the book called 1984. It is said that the desolate atmosphere of Jura is not totally strange in the desperation that permeates the novel.

Located in Craighouse, the only town on the island, where are also the church and the only warehouse, the distillery goes back officially to 1810 and was one of the first legal ones in Scotland. But clandestine distillers were undoubtedly settled there for a long time, especially in the grotto where they obtained the water used for the distillation. This water is marked by the aromas of peat that is not found in the malt. The current facilities date from 1958 and have experienced many modernizations. The distillery had stopped working since 1901. The breweries Scottish&Newcastle are the ones that have allowed this reconstruction, in order to provide some economic activity to the island, away from everything, and to make the blends of the Mackinlay brand. The production is really launched in 1963, and the «single malt» was commercialized from 1974. The distillery belongs today to the Invergordon group.

Without making his own malting, it makes a «single malt» very different from the island of Islay. Little peaty, quite clear, reminds a Speyside or a Northern Highlands malt. Nothing to do with the strong peaty and the iodized odors of malts from other islands.

The commercialization is based essentially on the ten years ones, which reproduces the silhouette of the island on its label. Its bottle has an original form in relation to many others. But there is also the twenty-six years, much rarer, with the name of «Stillman's Dram».

AND ALSO...

Imperial
Built in 1897, the year of Queen Victoria's diamond wedding (hence its name refers to the British Empire), this Speyside distillery has known long periods of interruption and many owner changes. The last one, Allied Distillers, uses it only for its blends; there are even bottles of «single malt» in the independent stores.

Inchgower
Installed in the northern port of Buckie, the distillery produces a whisky of fourteen years, marketed in the series «Flora and Fauna» of United Distillers group. It is classified in the Speyside category, its salty aromas and its very dry character are more related to coastal whiskies, even those of the islands.

Inchmurrin
One of the malts, the other the Old Rosdhu, produced by the distillery of Loch Lomond, on the southern limit of the Highlands according to a specific process (see «Loch Lomond») allow to make lighter alcohols. They serve mostly to obtain blends.

Inverleven
This Lowlands malt is made by the distillery of Dumbarton (Allied Distillers) according to the Lomond process. It was rarely bottled as «single malt» for independents sellers.

Islay Mist
It is one of the rare purest malts (or vatted malts) marketed today. Based on malts from Islay (Laphroaig, at least the original) and Highlands, it was prepared in 1928 for the twenty-first anniversary of the Lord of Islay, Lord Margadale. The brand currently belongs to the MacDuff group. There are two versions: luxury and seventeen years old.

The Jacobite
This standard blend was launched in 1983 by Nurdin&Peacock in the UK market for premier whiskies in mass distribution. Its name remembers the supporters of Jack II of England, the last king of the Stuart branch who was forced to went on the run in 1688.

King of Scots

Type: **blend.**
Origin: **Glasgow.**
Owner: **Douglas Laing.**
Date of birth: **1886.**

Returning to the end of the last century, this brand of blends has been reacquired by Douglas Laing around 1950, and has had a considerable development, especially in the export in the Far East and the Pacific area.

Originally, the blends were sold directly in casks to single buyers and bars. To serve it, they put it in jars or glass or ceramic bottles. This practice wanted to remember Douglas Laing presenting the King or Scots in a large collection of porcelain jars. There are many shapes, with or without a handle, round or hexagonal, or even remembering old Chinese jugs. The colors vary, from white to black to blue and dark red.

The assortment of decorations is also very wide, but the most typical is the rampant lion, heraldic symbol of Scotland, but also a superb sailboat, and the most precious bottles are decorated with gold of up to 22 carats. The King of Scots is also presented in cut-glass bottles, in small stubby bottles called maillets, and even classic bottles of 75 centiliters. Such variety is obviously conceived for luxury and duty-free shops, where these bottles are very appreciated gifts.

Inside these presentations, the assortment of blends was also quite broad, always in line with the style initiated by Douglas Laing: the young and light grain whiskies are joined with some little old malts from different regions of Scotland: Highlands, Lowlands and Islay.

Once the composition is made, it remains in casks for a few months.

The most common qualities are Rare Extra Old (eight to fifteen years old), twelve years old, De Luxe, seventeen years old and twenty-five years old. In each case, these ages indicate the malts of their composition.

Knockando

Type: **single malt.**
Origin: **Highlands (Speyside).**
Owner: **IDV (Grand Metropolitan).**
Date of birth: **1898.**

Installed on the banks of the River Spey, this distillery, whose Gaelic name means «small black hill», benefits exclusively from the waters of the Cardnach spring, of very good quality. Built in 1898 and enlarged after the Second World War, it is today the rosette of the IDV group, especially for its J&B blends. The current distiller, Innes Shaw, is the great-grandson of one of the builders of the original distillery.

When it was decided to develop and export the «single malt» in the late 70s, an original strategy was launched. Before setting a specific age (ten or twelve years, for example), the Knockando was bottled when the distiller estimated its apogee, between ten and fifteen years. The date (called here «station») is indicated on the label, which is rare in Scotland, as is the year of bottling. Without presenting large variations, the whiskies differ slightly from one date to another: the 1974 one is, for example, sweeter than the one in 1977, drier in the mouth. The departure of a new date is, since then, an event for fans and is carefully used for the promotion of the brand, especially abroad as it is widespread in more than fifty countries.

Although typical of Speyside whiskies, the Knockando is much paler than others, because no dye is added. Very soft and clear, it has complex aromas, with a very good finish. The use of a certain amount of sherry casks at the time of aging brings a subtle note of hazelnut. There is also a Knockando of more than twenty years, the Extra Old Reserve, presented in glass carafes, and much less common.

Knockdhu

Type: **single.**
Origin: **Highlands.**
Owner: **Inver House.**
Date of birth: **1893.**

At the foot of the hill of Knock, this distillery has many advantages: abundant springs, nearby inexhaustible bogs and the fertile plains of Laich O'Moray for the barley supply. The distillation allows at the time to give more work to the population. In the good season, the growers take care of the fields, then, once the harvest is done, they work during the winter in the distillery. Knockdhu was the first distillery created by the DCL group, in 1893, and the production was launched a year later. Such malt, much appreciated by blenders, has been long used only in the preparation of the Haig and only in very small quantities is available among the independents.

In 1983 the decision was made, apparently final, to close Knockdhu, due to the glut of «single malt» in the group.

But five years later, the Inver House group will buy and restart it. The two original stills were preserved, even the fuel surcharge was made manually. Modernized, the set of buildings has retained all the Victorian characteristics of origin. The group also decided to market the single malt specifically of twelve years, but then arose the problem of the almost similarity of the name and of «Knockando».

Also, it is the Gaelic term «An Cnoc», which has the same meaning as «Knockdhu», which finally was the one that designated the whisky. But for some time, there are the two denominations in the market. Coming from an area located on the edge of Speyside, the Knockdhu has malted and fruity characteristics, with a mild flavor. It is a great whisky to discover, since it has long been ignored in the market.

AND ALSO...

King George IV

This blend of the United Distillers group, destined mostly for export, bears the name and portrait of a king to whom Scotland and whisky owe a great deal. George IV moved to Edinburgh, in 1822, something that no British sovereign had done after at least two hundred years. He was received with great enthusiasm in the course of the ceremonies meticulously organized by Walter Scott to enhance Scottish traditions and folklore. Evidently, he savored numerous whiskies. This welcome and this finding considerably modified the attitude of London regarding Scotch whisky and the demand for legalization presented the following year by the Duke of Gordon was favorably received by the Royal Commission. Whisky could come out of hiding.

King Henry VIII

Appeared in 1953, this blend is made and marketed by a single man, Henry Stenham, which allows it to be sold at a fairly low price. It is found mostly in large distributors.

King James VI

Pertaining to an independent company, Forth Wines, it is a standard blend which its commercialization began in 1963 in the United Kingdom. Remember the memory of Maria Stuart's son, King of Scotland James VI, who became James I of England.

Lagavulin

Type: **single malt.**
Origin: **Islay.**
Owner: **United Distillers.**
Date of birth: **1816.**

In a small cove south of the island of Islay, well protected by the sea, in the Lagavulin site there were many clandestine distilleries in the eighteenth century, before legalization allowed their reunification into a single entity at the beginning of the following century. Not far from there are the ruins of the castle of Dun Naomhaig, stronghold of the lords of Islay.

The owners, the Graham brothers and their partner James Logan Mackie, are also the creators of the White Horse blend, of which Lagavulin malt is an essential element. The nephew of J.L. Mackie, Peter, who will make White Horse triumph, had learned the art of distillation in Lagavulin, which had been rather rare in the world of blenders. He even undertook the challenge of opening a second distillery in Lagavulin, called the «malt mill», where he experiments with original techniques, such as using peat as fuel for malting. But this facility was closed in 1962. Consequently, Lagavulin has followed the same story as White Horse, entering the DCL group in 1927.

Two characteristics undoubtedly explain the originality and quality of the Lagavulin malt: the water used remains for a long time in the neighboring peat bogs and the aging cellars are widely open to the sea air. Two characteristics that give its tasting: a first flavor quite dry, followed by an exceptional aromatic intensity with specific iodized notes, and an end marked by sherry.

Less overwhelming than its neighbor Laphroaig, Lagavulin whisky is often defined as «the aristocrat of Islay», both its balance and its exceptional body is the most representative of the island's whiskies. Such qualities deserve to be better known, and its introduction in the «Classic Malts» range of the United Distillers group was very justified to make it known to a large audience. The twelve years has been the first known, but occasionally leaves the position at the sixteen years old one, still more elaborate and more aromatic. Absolutely unclassifiable in the universe of Scotch whiskies.

The Lagavulin distillery, with its cellars on the edge of the sea.

Langs

Type: **blend.**
Origin: **Glasgow.**
Owner: **Robertson&Baxter.**
Date of birth: **1861.**

Hugh Lang founded in 1861, in Glasgow, a company specialized in the business of whisky and blending, quite old for Scotland. He was also an importer of rum. It was resumed later by his three children, Gavin, Alexander and William, who would continue with the activity. In 1876, the Lang brothers bought the Dungoyne distillery in the southern Highlands, which they renamed Glengoyne. The malts there became the basis of the composition of their blends. They developed with a constant care of quality and without creating any scandal, the business was of the family until 1965, date of its entry into the group Robertson&Baxter, also from Glasgow.

Nothing will change in any way in the initial strategy and style of the Lang brothers. The company takes advantage of an improvement in marketing, the stocks of the old most important whiskies and a unit in the barrel shop.

In addition to the Glengoyne malt, the range of Langs comprises two blends, considered classics of the genre. The Supreme Langs, composed about twenty-five whiskies at least five years old. The Langs Select, marked by a significant proportion of Speyside malts, is a twelve-year-old. The two are additionally aged, after the union, in oak casks for nine months.

Laphroaig

Type: **single malt.**
Origin: **Islay.**
Owner: **Allied Domecq.**
Date of birth: **1815.**

Laphroaig and Lagavulin have many points in common: the two distilleries are only a few kilometers away, on the south coast of Islay, and date from about the same time; their names have an almost similar Gaelic etymology. On the other hand, in the course of history, their leaders have had close relations: the Graham of Lagavulin have dealt with Laphroaig for a dozen years, after the death of its founder. Later they tried to copy Laphroaig, having fired their staff, then they were tempted to reacquire the distillery in 1921. And yet, they are different in the tasting. With all these similarities, the comparison between the two malts (even equally with those of Port Ellen and Ardber, equally neighbors) makes it clear that the skill of each distiller plays a key role in the production. Two brothers, Donald and Alex Johnston, built the distillery between 1815 and 1820, and it has not been almost changed afterwards. It still has its own malting facility, which is a good asset to preserve the characteristics of whisky, as well as the fact that the peat used has specific marine and iodine flavors.

In 1847, Donald, one of the founders of the distillery, drowned in a vat of whisky, which was particularly strange in history. Later, between 1954 and 1972, the distillery was run by a woman, Bessie Campbell (still very unusual in Scotland), arriving at the company as secretary.

The Johnstons were succeeded by the Hunters, their descendants, who claimed to maintain the reputation of the distillery despite numerous difficulties, especially financial ones. Laphroaig was purchased in 1967 by Allied Distillers, to ensure supply for the Long John blend.

Anyway, the notoriety of this whisky was already great. Also, in 1990, the leaders of Allied created a specific subsidiary, The Caledonian Malt Whisky Distillers, to market its range of «single malts» (Tormore, Miltonduff, Balblair), in which Laphroaig is the standard-bearer and produces the best sales. The Laphroaig has had the great merit of making discover the qualities of the Islay whiskies to the rest of the world and for this reason it has a clientele of diehard fans. It is true that its tasting allows us to appreciate all the originality: smoked aromas of great strength (some even say: medicinal) and marked by peat, iodine or also marine air. Some tasters find even tar tastes. His strength lacks a subtlety, but this makes Laphroaig a whisky unique in its kind.

The ten years is the most sold, but there is a fifteen year, very clear and harmonious.

On the other hand, the Long John, the Laphroaig malt, is the mainstay of the Islay Mist blend. In the remote island of Islay, the distillery has facilities allowing a good reception of the public. During the tour, visitors get all the information concerning the history and production of the whiskies.

Linkwood

Type: **single malt.**
Origin: **Highlands (Speyside).**
Owner: **United Distillers.**
Date of birth: **1821.**

This small distillery near Elgin, on the Lossie River, was created in 1821 by Peter Brown, a local businessman. His son will rebuild it completely in 1872, and knowing new facilities after the Second World War. In spite of this, its charm was preserved and constituted one of the most typical distilleries in the region.

This maintenance is largely due to Roderick Mackenzie, one of its directors from the 1930s, when the distillery entered the DCL group. In effect, it was his philosophy not to change anything in the buildings as a whole and not to make changes unless they were indispensable and that they were made with materials strictly identical to the originals. He considered that everything had its importance in the taste of his whisky and it was even forbidden to remove the cobwebs from the stores, in order not to modify the characteristics.

Used by Abbot's Choice et Checkers blends, Linkwood whisky was marketed equally in twelve years, in two versions. The general opinion was that it was the most representative of the Speyside style, with its notes of sherry, its slightly smoky aromas and its excellent general harmony. The version of the series «Flora and Fauna» marketed by United Distillers has very floral scents.

The independent bottlers have also older versions.

Lochnagar

Type: **single malt.**
Origin: **East Highlands.**
Owner: **United Distillers.**
Date of birth: **1825.**

Right after the legalization of the whisky, John Crathie, no doubt a clandestine distiller, settles at the foot of Mount Lochnagar. In any case, the current distillery dates from 1825 and was established by John Begg. The same year, Queen Victoria and Prince Albert bought the neighboring domain of Balmoral, to build a castle and make a residence in the Highlands.

The clever John Begg did not miss the opportunity to take advantage of such a neighborhood and, when the couple makes the first visit, in 1848, he invites them to his distillery; Prince Albert is preceded by a reputation for his interest in everything that has to do with mechanics. The couple arrives the next day and John Begg invites them to taste his whisky. He pleases them in such a way that a few days later he receives a privilege and can add the adjective of *real* to the name of his distillery, an exceptional reward that Lochnagar shares throughout Scotland only with Brackla. One can still ask if Queen Victoria really appreciated whisky, since she had the habit of mixing it with... her Bordeaux claret!

Such patronage will make the fortune of the distillery, so much so that the vacations of Queen Victoria in Balmoral encouraged the region a lot, especially in the month of September. The road that led from Aberdeen to Balmoral, which borders the river Dee, was called «Royal Deeside», attracting salmon fishermen and, on the other hand, skiers of the Grampian mountains. The place itself was commemorated by the poet Lord Byron, who underlined its wild and delicious character.

Such malt has also served to produce blends, such as Vat 69, or even the Begg, created by its owner.

For a long time reserved for the only real consumption and blending, Lochnagar whisky is now bottled as a twelve-year-old. It is sold mainly for export, especially in the duty-free warehouses of the Far East.

It is a very rich, complex and aromatic whisky, particularly mild. There is another version, the Selected Reserve, rarer, in which age is not specified. It depends on each bottle and is accompanied by a numbered that certificate its authenticity.

Long John

Type: **blend.**
Origin: **West Highlands.**
Owner: **Allied Domecq.**
Date of birth: **1825.**

If there is a legendary man in the history of whisky, that is Long John McDonald. It symbolizes perfectly the beginnings, sometimes difficult, of the Scotch whisky, and the enthusiasm that was necessary to impose his opinions.

John MacDonald belongs to an illustrious family, the MacDonald of Keppoch, whose origins go back to Robert I Bruce, king of Scotland in the fourteenth century. Two of his great-grandparents have distinguished themselves during the Battle of Culloden, the last attempt of the Scottish clans to oppose English power, in 1746. The defeat cost the MacDonald family dearly, because they lost a large part of their property.

Little John was born in 1746 into a family of rather poor settlers in the Highlands, where they illegally distilled a little whisky to improve their daily lives. In 1805, the family settled in Fort William, in the lands of the Duke of Gordon, and young John, unusual fact, receives a true education. At the time, they were putting into practice the way to exile the settlers, the nobles wanted to recover the land to raise lambs, something more profitable. One of John's brothers goes to the army, another goes into exile in Australia. As for John MacDonald, he remains a settler in the region. When he was twenty years old, he was 1.93 cm, which was a considerable size at the time and for this reason he was nicknamed «Long John». Its owner, the Duke of Gordon, was the author of the law legalizing the distillation of whisky, and Long John will turn to this activity, creating the first distillery in the region, called Ben Nevis, in 1825. At first he had to ask for money to be able to set up the business, he did not even have the license. He progressively managed to develop his business, starting as an exporter, although times were difficult. The summers of 1835 and 1836 were rainy and frozen, which caused the barley to be lacking, and even the peat was too wet

to be cut. In addition, the economic misery caused a drop in the consumption of whisky. In spite of everything, Long John could make appreciate his whisky, commercialized with the brand Dew of Ben Nevis, to the Queen Victoria, that kept a cask during fifteen years, just for the majority of age of the prince of Wales. Well known in the region, even throughout Scotland, Long John has left the memory of a man greatly appreciated, and his physical strength is the origin of many anecdotes: he saves the Duchess of Buccleuch, lost in the slopes of Ben Nevis, the highest mountain in Scotland, carrying with him a large bell that rang at regular intervals. He also shattered the neck of a bull that threatened one of his brothers.

He died in 1856, exhausted by financial difficulties. His business was healthy, as his son and successor Donald Peter distinguished himself. Sales multiplied by fifteen in less than ten years and a second distillery was built in 1876. At his death, in 1891, his business (whisky business and livestock) were inherited by his sons John and Archivald, who became progressively disinterested, to the point of selling the Long John brand, although retaining the distillery. The Long John blend underwent a great development after the Second World War, when it was bought back by the American group Schenley. The Ben Nevis distillery and the brand were again assembled in 1981, then joined the Allied Distillers group in 1989.

The standard blend, the most sold especially in the export, of twelve years, is marked by the use of a little malt Islay (Laphroaig). There is also a twenty-one-year-old, the Royal Choice.

Longmorn

Type: **single malt.**
Origin: **Highlands (Speyside).**
Owner: **Seagram.**
Date of birth: **1894.**

It is located in a place particularly suitable for distillation, the Lossie Valley in the Elgin region, where John Druff created Longmorn, a little later but at the same time as his neighbor Ben Riach. He had already

been a founder, some twenty years earlier, of Glen Lossie, located on the other side of the river. Then he had tried his luck in South Africa, then in the United States, and finally returned to Scotland. He wanted to take advantage of the boom that whisky sales were experiencing in the year 1890. But the trend changed, and the failure of a major blender, Pattison Limited, caused the ruin of John Duff.

Longmorn was retaken by a group of shareholders, its direction was entrusted to James R. Grant and then his two sons, nicknamed for this reason the «Longmorn Grant». It is true that this patronymic is very common in Scotland, and even more so in whisky centers. On the other hand, it remained in the same family until 1970; Longmorn then merged with the business of another Grant family, Glen Grant, who had created a group with The Glenlivet, before being owned by the Canadian group Seagram.

Local history claims that the site of Longmorn had been occupied for a long time by a chapel, and even an aging cellar occupies the site today. There was also a water mill, serving to grind flour, from the seventeenth century. At the moment, a paddle-wheel is visible in the distillery, although it is not very used for the production of energy. New stills were installed in 1972 and 1974 to cover the growing demand. The water here is particularly abundant and it is said that the spring, coming from the hill of Mannoch, will never run out. It is particularly peaty and gives its main characters to Longmorn malts. Wide and strong, with a lot of complexity and softness, they have always been very interesting for blenders, without being disdained by connoisseurs, quite the contrary. The name «Longmorn» has long been accompanied by the «Glenlivet» definition, — there is indeed a real kinship - and always appears in the bottles of ten and twelve years marketed by the distillery or independent bottlers (such as Gordon&MacPhail). After 1990, Seagram set out to develop its «single malt» in a specific range, «The Heritage Selection», in which Longmorn takes part. The fifteen years was preserved, wider and longer in the mouth, with a new bottle and label: the drawing of the distillery's place with a Celtic cross that perfectly looks like its religious past.

AND ALSO...

Label 5

This standard five-year blend bottled in Scotland has become the number one in the French market, thanks to the constant efforts of its distributor, La Martiniquaise. It is a perfect example of success supported by permanent advertising pressure and a good knowledge of large distribution networks.

Ladyburn

This Lowlands malt distillery was created in 1966 by the William Grant group, next to its Girvan grain distillery. The essentials of its production were used for the blends, but they are also held by independent bottlers. The distillery was closed in 1975.

Laird O'Cockpen

This brand of blend dates back to 1913 and refers to a great warrior of the fourteenth century, Sir Alex Ramsay of Dalhousie, Lord of O'Cockpen. It belonged to some blenders, Cockburn&Campbell, who had in Leith particularly cool cellars, ideal for aging and for conservation of their blends. The brand currently belongs to United Distillers.

Lauder's

This old brand of blend has seen its quality crowned by numerous medals throughout the nineteenth century. Purchased by MacDuff International in 1991, it is currently primarily intended for export.

Littlemill

Coming from a brewery, this Lowlands distillery, near Glasgow, is said to be the oldest in Scotland, with origins dating back to 1772. In any case, the current facilities date back to 1875. They have changed owner on numerous occasions, have closed for many periods and currently belongs to the Gibson International group. Littlemill sells an eight-year-old whisky.

Lochside

This old brewery of Montrose beers, on the west coast, was converted in 1957 into malt and grain distillery, especially making the Sandy MacNab's blend. It became the property of a Spanish group of spirits in 1973, specializing only in the production of ten-year-old Lochside whisky before it closed in 1992.

Logan

This luxury blend of twelve years is of White Horse (United Distillers), and simply bears the second name of its creator, James Logan Mackie, who made it known at the end of the last century. He was quite weird.

Lomond

This name of a lake in the north of Glasgow was also that of a malt still (which became very rare) and especially of a new type of still refining it in the late 50's. Equipped with a special cooling ring, was designed to produce very light whiskies, especially for the American market. Many copies were installed, especially in Inverleven, Glenburgie and Miltonduff by Hiram Walker. But the project was not very successful and many distilleries that used the Lomond still are currently closed or at a standstill.

Longrow

This Campbeltown whisky recalls the memory of an old distillery in this town that dates back to 1824. It is now produced by the Springbank distillery. It is a particularly peaty and strong whisky, close to Islay's.

The Macallan

Type: **single malt.**
Origin: **Highlands (Speyside).**
Owner: **Macallan.**
Date of birth: **1824.**

The name of this whisky particularly appreciated by the enthusiasts is preceded by the article *the* for about fifteen years, from the moment it began to be bottled. Therefore, unlike The Glenlivet, this is to distinguish it from other whiskies bearing the same mention, although it has a unique character in the world of whiskies. Because no one else resembles it, and the family that owns it for just over a century jealously defends its specific characteristics.

In the site where the distillery is located, on a hill overlooking the river Spey, there was a farm from the eighteenth century where clandestine distillation was practiced as in almost all the Highlands. It was legalized in 1824, one of the first in Scotland. The distillery changed owners many times before being acquired in 1892 by Roderick Kemp, a businessman who previously owned Talisker, on the Isle of Skye. Later, his two daughters and their husbands keep the control of it. To stand up to its expansion, the family company became a SA in 1968, but the descendants of Roderick Kemp owned the majority of the shares.

The Macallan owes its specificity to two reasons: the stills are of very small sizes (the smallest of all Speyside); aging is carried out entirely in casks of sherry, unique in Highlands, without any addition of caramel or other colorants.

Because of the growing rarity of these casks, society is forced after many years to buy some new barrels from Spain and make aging sherry (especially some of the more scent) for three or four years before using them for their malt. This increases the price of the casks ten times more compared to a bourbon cask. Later they will be only used once or twice at most, even aging in this same cask can last twenty-five, even fifty years. For a long time, this whisky, appreciated among the blenders, was little avail-

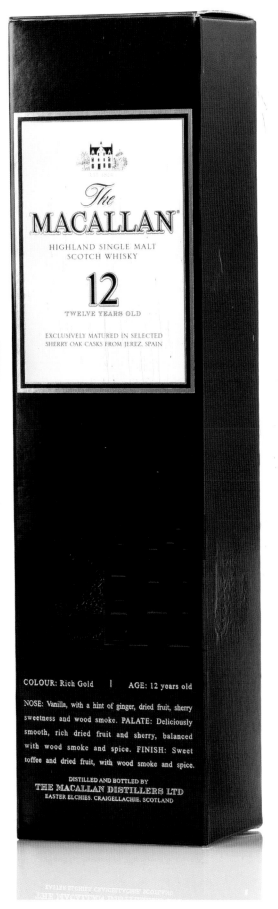

COLOUR: Rich Gold | AGE: 12 years old

NOSE: Vanilla, with a hint of ginger, dried fruit, sherry sweetness and wood smoke. PALATE: Deliciously smooth, rich dried fruit and sherry, balanced with wood smoke and spice. FINISH: Sweet toffee and dried fruit, with wood smoke and spice.

DISTILLED AND BOTTLED BY
THE MACALLAN DISTILLERS LTD
EASTER ELCHIES. CRAIGELLACHIE. SCOTLAND

able in bottles, except in some independent stores where they reached extraordinary prices. At the end of the 60s, the company launched the commercialization of «single malt» (which has been in the market since 1980) and proceeded to important research, doubling the capacity of distillation (but always with the same type of still). The distillery has a modern character.

It should be noted that the reference «Glenlivet» another time linked to the Macallan brand, today has disappeared.

There are few whiskies that generate as much discussion as The Macallan, not only between different ages, but also for certain harvest dates, which elicit comments as much as the great Bordeaux. It is true that the range is quite extensive: seven years (for the Italian market only), ten years (40 and 57°), twelve years, eighteen years and twenty-five years for the main ones, but there are many harvests (although the most appreciated are the 1950 and 1964). In 1993, the owner of a Japanese bar bought a sixty-year-old paying 50,000 francs for it.

The aromatic complexity of The Macallan really deserves to be discovered to understand the peaks that can reach a great Highlands whisky. The exceptional balance achieved by the aromas of malt and peat thus achieve an unparalleled long taste that makes it unmistakable, especially in blind tasting.

Despite the efforts of society to limit the phenomenon, certain independent bottlers propose other versions of Macallan, distributed by J.G. Thompson, whose age is not specified, and curiously named *As we get it.*

McGibbon's

Type: **blend.**
Origin: **Glasgow.**
Owner: **Douglas Laing.**
Date of birth: **1990.**

Golf was the favorite sport of the Scots, very proud to have invented it many centuries ago, and the idea of associating it with whisky occurred to the Laing brothers for a range of quite surprising blends, at least for its contents.

Reconstruct, in effect, in ceramic jars, a golf club, in a golf bag. The presentation is very curious; with Zip, buckles and pockets, they are collectibles that are very popular in duty-free warehouses, especially in the Far East. Each copy is numbered. Recently, some golf bags have been decorated with plaids of famous clans: Elliot (blue), McLeod (yellow), Dress Stewart (red) and Black Watch.

All these exist equally in miniature, with a more beautiful quality of realization.

The whiskies they contain are blends, the Premium Reserve and the Special Reserve, in the usual style of Douglas Laing: young grain whiskies associated with small amounts of old malts.

Finally, in 1995, McGibbon's launches a new collection of pottery jugs. They reproduce famous golf courses, such as St. Andrews or Turnberry, and the stopper, as you might guess, has the shape of a golf ball. This blend is called Master's Reserve.

Recall that is in this famous golf course of St. Andrews, located in the east of Scotland, where the rules of the game were first defined, and especially the number of holes (eighteen) constituting a route, without any definite reason.

They are whiskies to taste, as the slogan proclaims, «for the nineteenth hole», that is to say after the game. But, often, these jars do not have the same value uncorked, collectors give more value if they are intact, i.e. full.

Morthlach

Type: **single malt.**
Origin: **Highlands (Speyside).**
Owner: **United Distillers.**
Date of birth: **1823.**

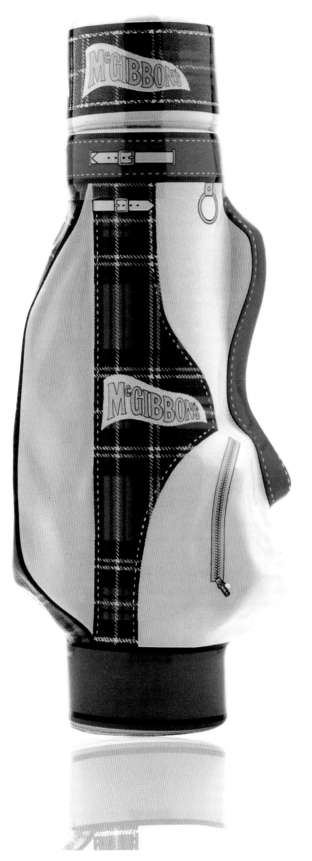

It is the oldest distillery in Dufftown, which currently has no less than seven. Its official creation dates from 1823, like the legalization of whisky, but there was a clandestine distillery after a long time. Because an excellent source, baptized «the well of John of Highlands», has been appreciated for a long time; it came from the hills of Conval, and not from the Dullan River that passes through Dufftown. After different owners, Mortlach was reacquired by George Cowie, who ensures the development even in London, and modernized it much in 1903. His son, a doctor who practices in Hong Kong, takes the succession and becomes a remarkable local highly esteemed. Then the distillery becomes part of the DCL group. For a long time reserved exclusively for the blenders, which are very much appreciated (especially for the Johnnie Walker), the whisky of Mortlach has been recently presented in a twelve year and a sixteen year, in the series «Flora and Fauna» of United Distillers. Typical of Speyside, this whisky is strong, very well balanced between smoked and malted, with long endings marked by sherry.

In 1995, Mortlach whisky was also marketed in a new range, the «Rare Malts Selection», created by United Distillers. Three old malts are used, between twenty-two and twenty-five years, removed from the casks without any reduction. In the case of Mortlach, a twenty-two-year-old participates with a 65.3-degree graduation. Some of these whiskies come from distilleries nowadays closed, such as North Port, Hillside or Glenlochy, and they are all particularly rare. They are perfect to taste after the meal, mixed with fresh water.

This initiative of the United Distillers group, which markets this range especially in the duty-free stores, marks a new stage in the knowledge of old whiskies. It develops a habit initiated for independent bottlers and amateur clubs, giving it more diffusion.

AND ALSO...

MacArthur's

Created in 1877, this blend belonging to Inver House underwent a renovation in 1970, being sold mainly in British supermarkets and then in French.

McCallum's

Dubbed «Perfection», this blend, created in 1911, recalls the name of two brothers, Duncan and John, famous for their pub and Edinburgh's wine and spirits shop, the Tattie Pit. Until the First World War, the whole Scottish aristocracy met there, but it was destroyed in 1916 by the only German bombing that hit the city. The blend, which currently belongs to United Distillers, has survived and has developed towards export, but also in the United Kingdom.

Mackenzie

This standard blend reference to a distiller installed in Perth after 1826, who was the owner of Blair Athol and Dufftown. The brand has been repurchased by Bell in 1933 and was sold mainly in some foreign markets.

Mackinlay

Nicknamed «The Original», this brand is named after a famous dynasty of wine and spirits sellers installed after 1815 in Leith, and which is currently at its fifth generation. Created in the middle of the last century, this blend appears today in Invergordon and exists in five, twelve and twenty-one years. It is very appreciated in the United Kingdom, but also in many other European countries for its smoothness and its production techniques.

Mannochmore

This Speyside whisky is made in a very recent distillery, built in 1971 near Glen Lossie. Produced exclusively to the creation of the Haig blend, it is also commercialized in the series «Flora and Fauna».

Martin's

This brand of standard and luxury blends is famous for many anecdotes. Its founder was a famous boxer before becoming a whisky entrepreneur. He wanted to call his standard blend «Martin›s VVO», he seized the vats of the Martini house, which had a name very similar to his, and in the end adopted the «James Martin's». appeal. In 1941 a cargo of James Martin's is lost when the ship, SS Politician, is shipwrecked on the Hebrides. This accident gives an argument for Compton Mackenzie to write a famous book, *Whisky Galore*; that becomes a particularly truculent film.

Miltonduff

This old Speyside distillery was built near an old brewery that was once very appreciated in Scotland. It has been many times completely modified, especially in 1890, in 1930 and in the 70s. It had many owners, and Hiram Walker was the one who put into practice the Lomond stills, to make the Mosstowie blend.

Currently belongs to the Allied Domecq group. The twelve-year-old whisky is both elegant, smooth and slightly peaty.

Oban

Type: **single malt.**
Origin: **West Highlands.**
Owner: **United Distillers.**
Date of birth: **1794.**

The port of Oban, on the west coast of the Highlands, was only a small fishing village when the Stevenson brothers landed there in 1778. They created many activities (slate quarries, naval constructions) before founding a distillery in 1794. Even restored many times after, it has keep its place in the center of town; It became very active with the trade of the islands. The panorama dominates a curious construction imitating the shape of the Coliseum, the Tower of McCaig.

The distillery was always of the Stevenson family until 1866, then it was owned by Walter Higgin, who enlarged it considerably. In the course of these works, they discovered a cave containing human bones that dated back to the Mesolithic period (between 10,000 and 3,500 BC). They are currently housed in a museum in Edinburgh, and the grotto has been carefully renovated.

At the end of the century, Oban became property of Aultmore, later it entered the Dewar group, and in 1930 it was transferred to DCL. It has never stopped working, a fact that has made it one of the oldest distilleries in Scotland that has always been active. For a long time, it has been dedicated to the production of blends, such as Old Mull of John Hopkins; Oban whisky began to be bottled in twelve years, then the fourteen years was introduced in the «Classic Malts» range of the United Distillers group.

Marked by the smoky touch, it is a whisky typical of the islands, very softly.

Old Parr

Type: **luxury blend.**
Origin: **Edinburgh.**
Owner: **United Distillers.**
Date of birth: **1871.**

Thomas Parr is a very famous historical figure in Great Britain, because he lived one hundred fifty-two years, between 1483 and 1635. Hence his nickname Old Parr. His life has been told in a famous writing by the poet John Taylor, published in the year of his death. He was called to the court of King Charles I, because the king wanted to ask the secret of his exceptional longevity. The old man replied that he had decided to do penance when he was one hundred years old, because he had committed adultery and had been condemned by the parish council. It is said that he married again, at the age of one hundred and twenty, and that he had a son. He met ten kings, and was represented in painting by Van Dyck and Rubens, then was buried, by royal order, in Westminster Abbey. Such longevity, with a name that was so well known in the United Kingdom, could not fail to inspire a brand of whisky. This was carried out in 1871 by two Ayrshire brothers.

However, it was above all in the export where Old Parr experienced the strongest growth. For a short time, it was owned by Alexander&McDonald, but in 1925 the brand was bought by the DCL group.

Made especially from Cragganmore and Glendullan malts, the Old Parr blend is a twelve-year-old powerful and smooth, presented in an old bottle of chunky shape, covered with cracks. There is also the Superior version.

Two specific containers were developed with the intention of entering the Japanese market and the duty-free stores: the Tribute, in a striking black bottle inside a luxurious box; the Elizabethan, the most expensive of the range (around 700 euros a bottle), presented in a superb case, also includes a complete and illustrated writing of the life of Thomas Parr. The glass bottle has four miniatures painted by hand and enhanced with decorations in tin. There have been a few hundred copies every year, all numbered.

Old Scots

Under his complete denomination «Rodgers Old Scots», this standard blend is named after a great businessman of the last century, who, associated with Thomas Slater, unveiled Scotch whisky in more than seventy countries. Later it is associated with Johnnie Walker. The blend is currently exported by United Distillers to the Middle East and South America.

Old Smuggler

This blend was created in the last century by two whisky dealers, the Stodart brothers, installed in Glasgow from 1835. Remember the clandestine distillers, famous for making better quality whiskies. The Stodart brothers were also reputed to have been the first to use sherry casks to bind it to their blends. It became the property of Hiram Walker, after Allied Domecq; the blend achieves the most important sales in the United States and Germany.

Passport

This blend, made by Seagram based on Glen Keith malt after 1968, is only sold for export, as its name suggests, with good results in the United States and in many European countries; sales exceed one million boxes per year.

Pig's Nose

With the slogan «Sweet and smooth like the snout of a pig», this blend of the Invergordon group has a not inconsiderable success.

Pinwinnie

This blend qualified as «luxury», but without age precision, was launched by the Inver House group destined essentially to the export markets. There is also a twelve-year version. Clear and light, it is marked by the sweetness of the Lowlands malts with which it is made in Airdrie.

Pittyvaich

Created in 1975 by the Bell Group in Dufftown, the distillery bottled a twelve-year single malt in 1991 in the «Flora and Fauna» series of the United Distillers group. But, later it has been closed.

Detail of a 19th century painting by John Frederick Lewis, *Highland Hospitality*.

Port Ellen

This Islay distillery, which dates back to the beginning of the 19th century, has been marked for a long time by the personality of its owner, John Ramsay. He was one of the first to consider the export of whisky to the United States, contributed greatly to the invention of continuous distillation created by Cooffey and Stein, and obtained from the government that the aging whisky did not have to pay fees.

After its demise, Port Ellen became the property of the DCL group. Closed in 1925, the distillery

was reopened in 1967, after important works, but again closed in 1983. Only the malt factory works, to produce Lagavulin and Caol Ila. Such malt is particularly hard to find.

Pulteney

The northernmost of the Scottish distilleries (with the exception of the Orkney Islands) dates back to 1826, but was very restored in 1959 by Hiram Walker. Such malt, with very marked marine aromas, is used essentially for the production of Ballantine's; small quantities are also available at independent stores.

Springbank

Type: **single malt.**
Origin: **Campbeltown.**
Owner: **J & A Mitchell.**
Date of birth: **1828.**

The history of Springbank refers to one of the saddest pages of the past of Scotch whisky, but it is also one of the most haughty distilleries in the country. The town of Campbeltown, located in the south of the island of Kintyre, was one of the great capitals of whisky, with up to twenty-two distilleries at the end of the last century, and still a dense of others in the county. Blenders across the country were particularly fond of these specific malts, and this may be what caused the fall of Campbeltown. Because most distillers, blinded by success, did not respect their quality parameters to supply malts in increasingly important quantities. The result did not take long to appear, and the blenders quickly moved away from their production. In 1934, only two distilleries remained, Springbank and Glen Scotia, always active. Founded in 1828 by a family, the Mitchells, who already had practice in the distillation after many generations, the distillery has not changed its owner, wanting to preserve its independence, maintaining the characteristic style of Campbeltown. There are only two distilleries in the area, and it has always been recognized as one of the four regions of Scotch whisky, along with Highlands, Lowlands and Islay. As found in Springbank malts, the Campbeltown style is marked by great marine freshness, is based on many elements. First, a specific distillation: after the classic double distillation, the heads and tails are again distilled, then mixed with brandy, giving them a greater depth. This method is very similar to the one practiced in Ireland, since the coasts are not more than thirty kilometers from Campbeltown. The absence of filtration for the cold, makes that the subtler components are better respected, but it entails a 46° bottleneck, which is on the other hand made in the same place, a unique case in Scotland together with Glenfiddich. Dyes, especially caramel, are rejected. On the other hand, when aging occurs, the assortment of bourbon or sherry casks causes marked differences in color and even taste and aroma. The place does the rest, because the island enjoys a very particular climate. Very marked by the maritime influences, it remains at the same time relatively temperate and above all very stable throughout the year, due to the action of Gulf Stream. The wineries, very exposed to the sea air, do not experience any thermal shock too important, and this gives a good harmony for aging.

To enhance the quality of its production, the Mitchell family has had, on the other hand, the cleverness of bottling a great variety of whiskies. Besides the Reserve, in which age is not indicated, there are also the twelve years, the fifteen years and the twenty-one years and, rarer, the twenty-five and thirty years. It is also found, especially in the distillery, many crops, such as 1958, 1962, 1965, 1967, 1972 and 1979. All have very interesting variations in colors and aromas, being true to the style: a salty sweetness allied to a subtle note of peat and marine air, including iodine. Which deserves the appeal of «first great classified soup» that was attributed by the *Times* of London in 1983. The distillation of Springbank also produces another whisky, Longrow, very different in style and aroma.

Strathisla

Type: **single malt.**
Origin: **Highlands (Speyside).**
Owner: **Seagram.**
Date of birth: **1786.**

The Strathisla distillery.

In the old town of Keith, on the island river, there is a brewery from the 13th century that was carried by monks, where the water was abundant and of good quality. In the late eighteenth century, a local businessman, George Taylor, decided to establish a small distillery, named after Milton. This name does not come from the old owner of the land, but from a nearby castle. The still was very small, according to the rules with the administration, but Taylor had the same difficulties with the treasury, since he also practiced an illicit distillation.

In 1828, the distillery was owned by William Longmore, an important businessman in the region who had obtained the passage of a line of railways, which provide an outlet to all local producers. Longmore modernizes the distillery, since a fire in 1876 and an explosion three years later caused great damage.

When the malt interests the blenders mainly, the dealer Gordon&MacPhail, of Elgin, obtains the right to sell a small quantity, under the name of Strathisla Glenlivet, and its fame begins to develop in the region.

At the beginning of the Second World War, the distillery was bought by a London financier, Jay Pomery, who, fraudulently, resold all stocks of malt destined... to the black market. But he did not escape from the British treasury and, since he could not pay the claim, his distillery was confiscated by the British State. It was repurchased by Chivas Brothers in 1950, which had entered the Seagram group a year earlier. A new era begins for Strathisla (which became definitely the name of the place), the group develops the distillery with new stills while retaining its old character. The picturesque place is very appreciated by tourists.

Such malt is the base of Chivas Real; independent bottlers continue to market at different ages (eight, fifteen, twenty and thirty-five years) and in many harvests.

Little peaty, smooth, the Strathisla is a whisky of great class, with some notes of sherry very appreciated. After 1990, the twelve-year-old was chosen to appear in «The Heritage Selection» range launched by Seagram, and benefits from a new bottle and a label that represents the distillery.

AND ALSO...

Rob Roy

This luxury blend, belongs to the Morrison-Bowmore company, is developed mainly for export, especially towards the market of France and Netherlands.

Rosebank

This great classic Lowlands malt is much appreciated by those who know it. Elaborated according to a triple distillation, it comes from an installation that goes back to the end of the XVIII century and later, in 1914, it becomes part of United Distillers. The distillery was halted in 1993, but in the market you can find (but for how long still?) the eight years, the twelve years and the fifteen years.

Royal Citation

The most recent of the Chivas Brothers blends is also one of the most complex. Five different types of casks are used especially for aging, in which the duration is not specified. It is presented in a recorded bottle.

Royal Salute

This premium blend of Chivas Brothers was launched in 1953 for the coronation of Elisabeth II. The term *royal salute* in effect designates a round of artillery in honor of an event that has to do with a member of the royal family. Quite rare, this blend comes in a porcelain carafe.

St. Magdalene

Interestingly, it is very strange that distilleries or Scottish markets make reference to religion. St. Magdalene was created in Linlithgow, in Lowlands, in a hospital bearing the same name, at the end of the 18th century. Despite the high qualities of its product, the distillery has been definitively closed in 1983, but it is still available from some resellers.

Scapa

The northernmost of the Scottish distilleries, next to Highland Park, is named after a large naval base installed on the Orkney Islands. Built around the year 1880, it has often been enlarged and has often changed ownership. Currently, it belongs to Allied Distillers, which uses the essentials of production for its blends. It is anyway possible to find the eight years and some harvests in the independent stores. They are very original, marked by both marine aromas and chocolate notes that come from the barrels of bourbon used for aging.

Scottish Leader

Produced by Burn Stewart, an independent group that has been repurchased by leading staff members in 1988, this standard blend undergoes a very important ascension, especially in mass distribution. There is also a twelve-year-old and a twenty-five-year-old, presented in a porcelain carafe.

Singleton

Recent distillery, dated 1974, Auchroisk is installed in the Speyside and its original architecture has won many awards. Created by IDV to respond to J&B's development desires, it only bottled its whisky in small quantities, with the name «The Singleton», since the name of the distillery, Auchroisk (which pronounced «othroysk»), is apparently too difficult for the uninitiated. It is an original whisky, little strong but with a great aromatic finesse.

Skye

This great northwest island has a distillery (Talisker) but it has also given its name to a range of blends. It was created more than a century ago by Ian MacLeod, the head of the original clan of Skye, from a union of different Islay and Speyside malts that age together in barrels for six months. The brand was reacquired in 1936 by a trading company of Edinburgh, Peter J. Russel Group,

which developed it strongly, especially in the export. In addition to the eight-year standard, the range has some twelve years and eighteen years old.

Speyburn

This distillery installed in a totally superb and typical site near Rothes, in Speyside, was created in 1897, the year of Queen Victoria's diamond wedding. For this occasion, a special barrel was produced and kept for a long time. This whisky has long been little bottled, the essentials of the production were available to blenders. But the Inver House group, which bought it in 1992, wants to develop ten-year marketing first and foremost.

Speyside

Taking the name of one of the most famous regions of malts, this blend was launched in the 50s by George Christie, who also created a brand of pure malt, Glentromie. It has been many years before he was able to re-open a malt distillery, Drumguish, located on the River Spey, in Kingussie, which had been closed after seventy years. The production of Drumguish began in 1993 and it is still too early to estimate its qualities.

Stewart's Cream of the Barley

Originally created by a Dundee dealer, Alexander Stewart, this standard blend belongs to Allied Distillers from 1969, and it's presented in an original bottle, reminding a little of those used after shaving. It is quite widespread in the United Kingdom and in many countries in Europe.

Strathmill

This distillery of Keith (Speyside), more than a century old, belongs today to IDV, and serves mainly for the elaboration of the J&B. Some independents marked the whisky.

Talisker

Type: **single malt.**
Origin: **Skye.**
Owner: **United Distillers.**
Date of birth: **1830.**

The island of Skye, the largest of the Hebrides archipelago, has only this distillery, tucked in the Harport inlet. In addition to its romantic and very picturesque landscapes, Skye is loved by all the Scots, because it was a last refuge for his hero, Bonnie Prince Charles, the last of the Stuart suitor to the crown. Many inhabitants still speak Gaelic, and the island has long had its own currency, the unit was equivalent to a working day in the distillery. Two sons of a doctor from the island of Eigg, Hugh and Kenneth MacAskill, implanted the distillery in 1830, after many unsuccessful attempts. They had rented the site to the MacLeod clan, the most important on the island. Although the owner, Hugh, was not nearly appreciated in the region, because he expelled the settlers to develop lamb farming. But he was pardoned when he helped the famine victims of 1840. Inspired by the Irish, the MacAskills made their malts with a triple distillation, a technique that was maintained until 1928.

There have been many owners, with some disappointments at times, one of them went bankrupt for having sold stocks of whisky... that had never existed. In 1880, Talisker became the property of two partners, Grigor Allan and Roderick Kemp, who made numerous investments and developed the notoriety of the already well-known malt: in a poem of the same year, R.L. Stevenson wrote: «The queen of drinks, as I conceive it, is from Talisker, Islay or Glenlivet». Kemp leaves Talisker in 1892, to buy back Macallan, and Allan then acquires Dailuaine; continuing to invest in the island, especially in a loading dock and many buildings. In 1925, his company merged with the DCL group, and his malt served especially for the production of Johnnie Walker. In

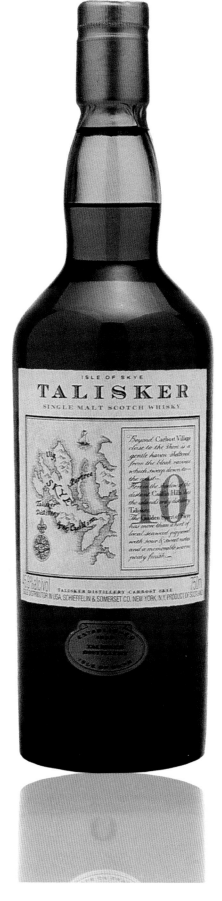

The Talisker distillery on the Isle of Skye.

The creation of this Speyside distillery (such as Knockando and Imperial) owes much to the arrival of a railway line to Craigellachie that allowed the transport of whisky. The place was known since time immemorial by clandestine distillers for the abundance and quality of the water. It dominates the valley of the Spey, a particularly picturesque narrow area.

William Grant, director of Highlands Distilleries, spent a lot to create the installation, calling the best engineer of the time, Charles Doig, who made a distillery considered the most modern of his time. Its distance from the nearest town made it necessary to build housing for the workers and even an access to reach the main road.

In the railway line, was created a station especially for the distillery, with the name of Dalbeallie. When the railways ceased to exist, the station was preserved under the name of Tamdhu, which today houses an information center for the visitors of the distillery.

The success was sudden and the distillery quickly increased its production in the first years. Immediately it lived the up and downs of the market, since the essentials of such malt were destined for blenders, especially for The Famous Grouse. Tamdhu had to close for about twenty years from 1928.

After the war, its launching was a rocket,

1960, a violent fire destroyed the main part of the distillery and he replaced the five stills with copies that faithfully reproduce the lost originals. Only the original capacitors could be saved. The malting, on the other hand, was suppressed in 1972. Talisker produces a slightly unclassifiable malt, even if it is mixed sometimes with those of the island of Islay. Undoubtedly it has the strength, so impressive at the beginning of the tasting that someone even speak of a volcanic character, making unconsciously reference to the mountains that surround the distillery. It also reveals some very peaty aromas, but its spicy notes and its malted sweetness are very characteristic, as well as a marine freshness. It is bottled at 45.8°, which is quite exceptional compared to usual practices. For a long time, the eight years has been the only one available, but since Talisker entered the «Classic Malts» range, there is the ten years that has been broadcast, and its label bears an old map of the Isle of Skye.

Tamdhu

Type: **single malt.**
Origin: **Highlands (Speyside).**
Owner: **Highland Distilleries.**
Date of birth: **1897.**

The old Tamdhu railway station has been preserved.

with such success that it had to double the capacity in 1972 to add two new stills.

The commercialization of «single malt» dates from 1976, and is mainly made by a ten year, but also a fifteen year. It is a whisky very representative of Speyside, full of balance and elegance, very harmonious and perfumed. It is often recommended to the neophytes in the matter of whisky, because, without becoming cloying, makes immediately discover the breadth and aromas of a large whisky.

Teacher's

Type: **blend.**
Origin: **Glasgow.**
Owner: **Allied Domecq.**
Date of birth: **1884.**

William Teacher was a young man who did not lack ambition. He entered in 1830 as a simple clerk in a small shop on the outskirts of Glasgow, quickly married the employer's daughter, then persuaded his father-in-law to obtain a license as a spirit's trader. He became a wholesale seller in 1850, specialized in both selling at the store and at the pubs where only whisky was sold, the *dram shops*. Helped by his two sons, Adam and William, he was the most important store owner in Glasgow, possessing almost twenty of them.

At the beginning, his sons specialized especially in the techniques of the blending and the assembly of the whisky. They get good results, so much so that their whiskies will not only be sold in family stores, but also in other distributors in the region. They were able to produce «custom-made» blends, according to the wishes of the retailers.

In 1884, the blend made the family kneaded a fortune, the Teacher's Highland Cream. With the proportion of malts more important than what is usually used, they create a new category, the premium blends. On the other hand, to ensure their malt supplies, the Teachers built their own distillery in Speyside, Ardmore, in 1897-1898. Later, in 1960, the company will acquire another distillery in the region, Glendronach.

In 1913, one of Adam Teacher's nephews invented the cap with capsule (at the time in wood, today in plastic), which allowed to open a bottle without resorting to the corkscrew. Teacher's will be the first whisky that will take advantage of this innovation, that was very beneficial for their sales. The descendants of William Teacher assured for a long time their independence, resisting especially to the attacks of the group DCL in the 20s. In any case they ended up being absorbed by the group Allied Distillers in 1976.

Té Bheag Nan Eileam

Type: **blend.**
Origin: **Skye.**
Owner: **sir Iain Noble.**
Date of birth: **1976.**

Endowed with an unpronounceable name for those who do not speak Gaelic, this blend nevertheless owes its success to the use of this language. In phonetics, this is «chay vek nan eelan», and means «little lady of the islands», an affectionate term used in Scotland, especially to designate a small glass of whisky.

It was launched by Sir Iain Noble to resurrect the economic activity of his people, Isle Ornsay, a small port on the south coast of the Isle of Skye. Its prosperity was severely affected by the arrival of the railroad to another town, this involves the transfer of ferry-boat lines, damaging many islands in the region. At first, only the brand was written in Gaelic, but a bard recommended to Sir Noble that his whisky would gain much in quality if the entire label was in this language, and that is what he did. Precisely because of this it is practically the only one that bears the mention of *«uisge beatha»*, the old Gaelic term that gives birth to the word «whisky». This original label contributed greatly to the success of the brand, not only in the whole region of the Hebridean Islands, where the Gaelic is still spoken, but in the export, because the immigrants were very satisfied to be able to display a bottle in their language. In 1978, Sir Noble launches a second brand, Poit Dhubh, which is pronounced «Pot-Doo», and which means «the black cauldron», a term that designated the still in the smuggling era. It is a «pure malt» of twelve years, born by the union of different malts of the islands and Highlands, which will probably be a bit of Talisker, the only one of the Isle of Skye. It has the same success as the Té Bheag. Además. In addition, Sir Noble has also opened a trading school on Ornsay Island (or Eileann Iarmain, in Gaelic) where the rules of marketing and selling are taught... in Gaelic!

Tobermory

Type: **single malt.**
Origin: **Mull.**
Owner: **Burn Stewart.**
Date of birth: **1798.**

Located at the northern tip of the Isle of Mull, west of Scotland, the distillery owes to its distance the uncertainties that have shaken its existence after almost two centuries. It was founded in 1798 and legalized in 1823. Its creator, John Sinclair, established it in the port where it owned an important flotilla, which allowed him to bring the barley from Highlands and issue his whisky. A particularly aromatic water for its passage through the peat bogs gives it a very characteristic taste. In 1863, when Sinclair died, the distillery entered a period of deferment for some thirty years, which was followed by many more, and it met different owners, including the DCL group, but, apparently, the isolation of the distillery discouraged many interested. Reopened in 1972, the distillery is renamed Ledaig and the new owners make major renovations. But the whisky market was not very favorable during this period, and the distillery changed owner again seven years later, before closing for about ten years until 1990. The commercialization of Tobermory's production underwent numerous variations, something that helps a lot the fan to find it again. In addition to «single malt», where age is not specified, there is also a «pure malt» and even a blend of the same brand. On the other hand, the Ledaig brand has been marketed, especially the eighteen years in crops.

Since 1993, Tobermory has joined the group Burn Stewart and hopes to make this quite special whisky survive, rather light but aromatic. It is marketed in a pale green screen-printed bottle, an unusual presentation in the matter of whisky. Despite its distance, the distillery deserves to be visited, because it has not been changed since its creation, nor has the port of Tobermory.

Tomatin

Type: **single malt.**
Origin: **Northern Highlands.**
Owner: **Takara Shuzo&Okura.**
Date of birth: **1897.**

Located about twenty kilometers south of Inverness, the Tomatin distillery is the most important in Scotland with its twenty-three stills, and one of the largest in the world after that of Suntory in Japan. Curiously, on the other hand, it has become the property of a Japanese consortium...

Its creation in 1897 by many businessmen of Inverness was related to the growing sales of whisky at the time. The chosen site was near a very old farm where clandestine distillers once lived. The water is very abundant and is aromatized in the peat bogs before being used for distillation.

The rise of Tomatin's power was very progressive, and it was not until the 50s when it was at full capacity. At its maximum capacity, in the 70s, it produced up to 22 million liters of malt, used by numerous blenders throughout Scotland. Very automated (two workers were dedicated to operate the set of the stills), the installation seemed more a refinery than a classic distillery. To save energy, a part of the hot water is recovered to breed eels and trout.

Listed on the Stock Exchange, the company has had shareholders such as the Heineken breweries. But the difficulties of the whisky market in the 1980s have unleashed many problems for Tomatin, despite a progressive reduction in production.

It was finally liquidated in 1985, but its importance complicated the search for new shareholders. Even for the Japanese giant Suntory it was difficult to control so much production capacity. Finally, the Japanese companies Yakara Shuzo&Okura, which had previously been importers of Tomatin whisky, acquired it in 1986. They were the only ones that could make

such an investment. Despite its vocation to supply the blenders, Tomatin also bottled a ten year and a twelve year. Fresh and clean, this whisky is quite sweet and smooth, a little smoky. It is mainly found in a blend made by the distillery, the Big T, which reflects its importance quite well. Tomatin also produces a blend of twenty-one years, curiously called Old St. Andrews, since Scotland's oldest golf course is on the opposite side of the distillery on the east coast.

Tomintoul

Type: **single malt.**
Origin: **Highlands (Speyside).**
Owner: **Whyte&Mackay.**
Date of birth: **1964.**

Despite its modernity, this distillery built in early 1964 produces a whisky within the great tradition of Glenlivet, the region where it is located. Anyway, it is not exactly on the edge of the River Livet, but on the banks of the Avon, which receives the waters. It is one of the highest distilleries in Scotland, and the town is located in an exceptional site for lovers of climbing and hiking, especially in the direction of the Cairn Gorm mountains, which are close to 1,300 meters.

As is common in the region, the place has been occupied on many occasions by clandestine distillers, a logical explanation because of the abundance of water that exists there. The town belongs to the parish of Glenlivet and, on its label, the brand clearly flaunts its relationship in the standard. Ten years after its creation, Tomintoul began to bottle its own whiskeys, an eight-year-old and a currently ten-year-old, but there are also a twelve-year-old. They all follow the style of The Glenlivet, with its characteristic aromatic finesse. This may be the lightest of all, with a lot of sweetness, but with a lot of body, which is noticeable in the long run.

Tormore

Type: **single malt**.
Origin: **Highlands (Speyside).**
Owner: **Allied Distillers.**
Date of birth: **1959.**

It is the first distillery built in the twentieth century in the Highlands, and therefore has an elegant and slightly old-fashioned style, which gives it an air of spa of the last century. The imposing building, designed by the architect Albert Richardson, president of the Royal Academy, has harmonious proportions and combines white and gray in a very good way. A watchtower equipped with a carillon and a small lake with some

pumps complete the set, something that astonishes a little in this place a bit far from Speyside.

Located next to the confluence of the Spey and Avon rivers, the distillery is nourished by the very pure and very cold water of the Achvochkie spring, of which it has exclusive use. This water comes from the hills of Cromdale, where it is aromatized in the peat bogs.

At the beginning it was built to respond to the needs of Long John malt, as proudly proclaimed by a plaque at the entrance, the Tormore distillery also bottles its whisky, and the current is a ten year one, but there is also a twelve year for some markets from exportation.

It is a very elegant whisky, following the Speyside style, which shows that it is not

necessary for a distillery to be centennial to be a perfect classicism. Its balance and its softness are extremely pleasant, with notes of honey and a smoky touch.

The Tormore distillery was built in the late 50's.

AND ALSO...

Tamnavulin

Built in 1966, this distillery is the only one, next to The Glenlivet, which has been installed on the shore of the Livet River, when others were recommended to be located a few kilometers away.

Its malt is very pale (no cask of sherry is used for aging), it is very aromatic and of a great balance, within the style of its famous neighbor.

Tantallan

This brand of Highlands malt belongs to a new society, the Vintage Malt Whisky, created in Glasgow in 1992, which offers us some others whiskies: Finlagann (Islay), Glen Andrew, Glen Almond or even Tambowie, with the name of an old distillery destroyed in 1920, and that society seeks to rebuild. The most surprising thing about Vintage Malt Whisky is that sometimes the labels mention «single malt», when none of their whiskies come from a single distillery, as required by tradition, or legislation, since they make their blends.

Teaninich

This distillery of the Highlands of the North, whose name is pronounced «Chee-an-in-ick», has existed since 1817. After many independent owners, it enters the DCL group. It is since 1992 when his whisky of ten years is bottled in the distillery. Pale and perfumed, it is a very distinguished whisky.

Tullibardine

For a long time, the buildings of this Blackford distillery have housed a brewery, famous since the late Middle Ages. The transformation dates back to 1949. It became the property of the Invergordon group in 1992, the distillery bottles two whiskies, a ten-year strong and a twenty-five year, known as the «distiller's cup» (Stillman's Dram).

The Tullibardine distillery was originally a brewery.

UNITED DISTILLERS

When, in 1827, Robert Stein, a distiller from the Lowlands, invented a still for continuous distillation, improved three years later by Aeneas Cooffey, tax man in Dublin, neither of them realizes that they had just revolutionized the world of whisky

Since its apparatus allows to distil easily large quantities of liqueur without having to empty or reload the still. For the history, it is necessary to remember that Aeneas Cooffey proposed at first his invention to the Irish distillers, but they didn't like it, then he went to make the demonstration to the Scots, who hurried to use it.

For a few decades, grain distillers wanted to become important, so much so that, in 1853, Andrew Usher of Edinburgh marketed a first blending whisky. The innovation was approved in 1860 by the Spirits Act, which authorized the mixing of different whiskies without additional fees. As a result, it was more interesting to sell blended whiskies, where grain whisky plays an essential role in obtaining a less expensive resale price.

The growth of the market is such that it makes the distillers join together. They reached a first commercial agreement in 1856, then a second in 1865, to protect their interests and reduce their expenses. In April 1877, there are finally six distillers merged into the same company, the Distillers Company Limited (DCL), with the blessing of public powers: MacFarlane, Bald, Haig, Macnab, Mowbray and Stewart. This society, which was even listed on the stock exchange, aroused many envies, which led some blenders and businessmen to create a rival company, the North British, in 1885.

FROM GRAIN TO MALT

DCL is not limited only to grain whiskies and builds its first malt distillery in 1893, in Knockdhu. It is the time of the great whisky boom. Sales are growing tremendously,

especially in the blends, and whisky is fashionable all over Britain.

A scandal stopped this prosperity a little. The Pattison brothers, of Leith, are the kings of the time. Encouraged by the banks, they sold large quantities of whisky backed by advertising. They installed 500 parrots in the bars of London, which repeated incessantly: «Drink Pattison whisky».

But the Pattison, to meet the demand, tricked the quality of their whisky. In 1898, were accused of fraud and went bankrupt.

The scandal was huge and especially generated a chain reaction, as many distillers and even blenders were dependent on the Pattison. Only DCL had sufficient financial means, and it was dedicated to buying little by little the businesses. Although at the beginning of the century the whisky market went down again.

Seeking a good reaction, the malt distillers wanted to appropriate the monopoly of the term «whisky», and denied its use to the blenders. They won the first trial in 1906. DCL made a great ruckus with the support of the blenders, and obtained three years later the official recognition, that both grain or malt made a good whisky. The war allowed DCL to increase its power. Since a stream of puritanism and anti-alcoholism emerged from 1915 in Britain. Without reaching the prohibition, this triggered a strong growth of rates in relation to whisky. And, as the American market was hit by the ban, sales declined both in the interior and in the export.

Both distillers and independent blenders could not resist, and were forced to close, or associate as DCL. At the end of the 20s, the company controlled all the major brands of the time and one third of the Scottish distilleries.

A DISCUSSED PREEMINENCE

From before the Second World War, rivals

appeared, coming especially from Canada (Hiram Walker). But the global conflict paralyzed the situation, both in low consumption and in the difficulties of supplying cereals.

From the 50s, the threats against the supremacy of DCL were confirmed. With Seagram, North America confirmed its pretensions in the whisky market. On the other hand, blenders brands developed, such as J&B, Bell's, Chivas or Teacher's, covering the British market, and overshadowing the DCL brands.

This reaction was due to a policy of falling prices, when the market did not cease

A bottling center of the United Distillers group.

to develop: the production of grain whisky was multiplied by four between 1959 and 1966. New distilleries were created and others increased their production capacities. But the coup of Jarnac would come from Brussels and the EEC. It rebuked DCL in December 1977 for its tariff practices. In effect, they did pay the same expensive whisky to their continental distributors than to the British market. For DCL, these was a means of remunerating the efforts of their distributors to develop their brands and to prevent the emergence of a parallel market.

An old Edinburgh pub, near the castle.

But this contravened the community rules.

Also DCL won the lawsuit, six years later, but it was necessary to obey in the meantime. The alternative was to withdraw some leading brands from the British market, such as Johnnie Walker Red Label and Dimple, and increase the prices of other brands to make them uninteresting for the parallel market. In short, the distribution of some brands was entrusted to Whyte&Mackay in the British market.

Despite DCL's attempt to create new brands for the United Kingdom (John Barr, Buchanan's), its market plots were greatly diminished. And mainly, the whole thing showed its weakness. Nothing surprising after the giant became the object of greed.

In December of 1985, the group of supermarkets Argyll tries to buy DCL. Its purpose fails, but this operation weakens the group more. Then Guinness enters the scene.

This beer giant had acquired the previous year Bell. After some vicissitudes, they won the battle in May 1986 and thus became the first world group in the beverage sector. The Scottish distillers lose their independence, becoming more specific for the change of name: DCL becomes United Distillers.

There remains a fabulous portfolio of brands, (more than a hundred) including the world number one, Johnnie Walker. This new transfer implies an improvement in the perception of market developments. Noting the new demand for «single malts», United Distillers launched the range of its six «Classic Malts», valuing some of its jewels such as Lagavulin or Talisker and initiating a movement that will be taken up by other groups in the sector. Even following the example of independents such as Glenfiddich and Glenfarclas, United Distillers develops a great policy of opening its distilleries to visitors, thus favoring tourism that benefits the whole country. Although the group no longer occupies the majority position of years ago, United Distillers, for its connections in the world market of spirits, will always retain an irreplaceable place in the world of whisky.

Usher's

Type: **blend.**
Origin: **Edinburgh.**
Owner: **United Distillers.**
Date of birth: **1853.**

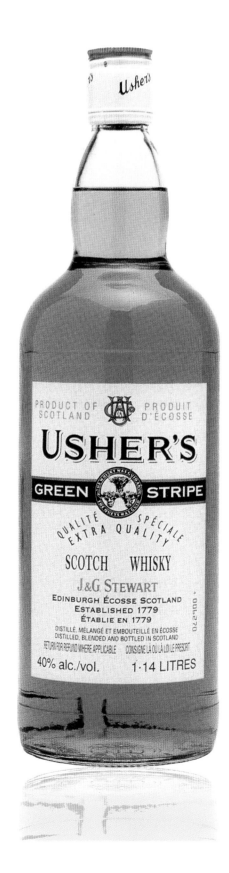

We owe it to the Usher father and son, the two named Andrew, to have contributed to the whisky with its development. Born in a family of wine and spirits dealers, the first Andrew Usher obtained exclusivity from the sale of The Glenlivet in 1840. On the other hand, he had understood the importance of aging to increase the quality of whisky and created some wineries to be able to have a stock and make it age in good condition. At the same time, he became interested in mixing different whiskies. The practice was not new, but he adopted a scientific mode for this purpose, knowing that the final result exceeded the simple addition of the different components. He would start by creating a «pure malt» (or still *vatted malt*) called Old Vatted Glenlivet, solely based on «single malts» from Glenlivet.

The new fiscal legislation adopted in 1860 prompted one of his sons, also named Andrew, to go further by uniting the malt and grain whiskies. At first, he reduced the costs, because grain liqueur was cheaper. But the end result was also revealed to be more pleasant, and easy to market in Britain.

Success is predictable and Andrew Usher's magic formula would be imitated a lot, making the blend the true locomotory of Scotch whisky not only in London but throughout England, but also in the whole world.

Andrew Usher and his brother John knew how to handle their success, their brand became one of the first to export outside the United Kingdom. They would also be the origin of the creation of the North British, an attempt by the distillers to counteract the power of the DCL. Generous benefactors of the people of Edinburgh, the Usher could not prevent their society from being forced to merge with DCL in 1919. Their brand, with its famous green band, would continue to exist, especially for export to South America and some European markets.

Vat 69

Type: **blend.**
Origin: **Leith.**
Owner: **United Distillers.**
Date of birth: **1882.**

The whisky has been able to generate some characters, and William Sanderson is surely part of these. Born in Leith, he started out in the business world in 1863, twenty-four years ago, as a «maker of wines and spirits», that is, as a blender, and will be one of the first to develop and market blends.

In search of the best blend formula, one day he came up with the idea of making a hundred of them and submitting them, in July 1882, to the judgment of friends and colleagues. The number 69 is the one that would be designated like winner and, without looking for more, it began to be commercialized by Sanderson with the name of Vat 69. It does not mean, however, the pope's personal telephone number (VAT for... Vatican), which is a very widespread story in British pubs.

It is unknown exactly what conditions this historical tasting took place, and what state the tasters were in (although after having taken a hundred whiskies...), but the most surprising thing about the story is that Vat 69 had a real success that even today it is still not understood, being among the fifteen top brands of whisky sold in the world.

William Sanderson did not stop here, he continued with his searches, trying other combinations and blends recipes. Some years later, he did the same operation as with Vat 69, designating a Vat 88... which had almost no future.

His son, then his grandson, continued with the exploitation of the brand, buying many malt distilleries. After an alliance with the gin producer Booths, his society was forced to merge in 1937 with DCL, but retaining his personality, and above all the precious family recipe.

And the descendants of William Sanderson have continued to carry the family brand for many generations, obtaining in 1967 a «Queen's Award» for export.

White Horse

Type: **blend.**
Origin: **Edinburgh.**
Owner: **United Distillers.**
Date of birth: **1883.**

The white horse, emblematic figure of the Scotch whisky, even of a whole British symbolism that is found especially in the label of many pubs, was born in the fertile brain of James Logan Mackie. This blender installed in Edinburgh distinguishes himself from its peers by its interest in distillation techniques, and especially those of Lagavulin, on the island of Islay. The local malt, famous for its strength, gave a lot of character to the blend that Mackie invented in 1883.

To give it a name, it is inspired by a hostel with this sign in Cowgate, near Edinburgh, which was used for a time as the diner of officers of Bonnie Prince Charles. The name «White Horse» has many explanations. Remember the horse that rode Marie Stuart, Queen of Scotland. But it is also the heraldic emblem of the house of Hanover, and the pubs that took this name proclaimed in this way their political allegiance. It is even said that the lodge had been baptized in memory of a white horse that, during a legendary race, achieved victory, saving its owner from bankruptcy. There are a thousand stories surrounding «White Horse» to satisfy the British imagination. Mackie began to market his blend, and mentioned in the label «Founded in 1742», that it is not the date of creation of the brand or of this society... but it is the famous hostel of Cowgate. One detail, no doubt... The fate of White Horse is in the railways and the brand will be more than developed by Peter Mackie, the nephew of the creator and his successor from 1900.

Nicknamed «the Restless», it wastes a lot of energy to promote whisky. To every piece of advice for prudence, their response is «nothing is impossible», which was the motto of their society. His commercial network was widespread, becoming a class model, and Mackie's favorite observation was to say no matter where on the globe: «If you can get there, you'll find White Horse». At the same time, this aggressiveness is duplicated with another great success: after having bought many distilleries, he would be a fierce militant of the lengthening of whisky aging, convinced that the improvement of quality is still the most effective weapon for its survival and its success among consumers.

Old White Horse bottles and, below, the Craigellachie distillery, which makes the base malt of the White Horse.

Whyte & Mackay

Type: **blend.**
Origin: **Glasgow.**
Owner: **Whyte&Mackay.**
Date of birth: **1882.**

The First World War contributed to the prosperity of their businesses and the White Horse became the favorite whisky of many garrison officers. When Peter Mackie died in 1924, his company remained true to his cleverness, developing from 1926 a revolutionary screw capsule, thanks to which White Horse multiplied its sales. Anyway, although Peter Mackie resisted the DCL attacks for a long time, his society would be forced to merge in 1927. Something that would not prevent White Horse from continuing to occupy one of the top positions in the world whisky market.

When Charles Mackay and James Whyte created their whisky society, they already had solid experience in the field; Mackay had worked for Allan&Poynter. From its beginnings, in 1882, they launch their blend, Special Reserve.

Progressively, society became one of the most important in Glasgow for blending. Two sons of James Whyte reunited Whyte&Mackay in the 20s, but the company had already become SA. The export in the 30s, after the growth in the British market after the Second World War, allowed them to develop.

In 1960, they merged with Mackenzie (Dalmore), then bought other distilleries (Tomintoul, Fettercairn). The group was in 1972 owned by a financial company, Scottish&Universal Investments; then, in 1990, by Gallaher, a subsidiary of the powerful American group American Brands (which also controls Jim Beam), and who was already the agent of Whyte&Mackay in the United States.

Having taken advantage of the recovery of many DCL brands in the British market and export, Whyte&Mackay also attracted attention for their innovations, such as a special metal capsule that also served as a dosing cap. They also released the magnum, which became a classic in whisky bars. These innovations, accompanied by a sponsorship policy in football and golf, allowed the brand to conquer one of the first positions in the Scottish market, particularly in Glasgow. Its concern for quality is evident, especially in the development of its blends. To give them more depth and aromatic complexity, the malts and grain whiskies were first aged separately in a few casks of sherry; the mixture was not made until after a few months.

Before the final mixture, they experience a second period of maturation. In addition to the Special Reserve, Whyte&Mackay proposes a luxury version and a twenty-one year.

William Lawson's

Type: **blend.**
Origin: **Dundee.**
Owner: **William Lawson.**
Date of birth: **1849.**

William Lawson created in 1849 his society of whiskies; after a few years, he launches his own blend with his name. But the brand was quite modest for many years. Its real takeoff began with the arrival of the Martini&Rossi group, which began exporting the blend.

The power of the sales network in the world and its marketing capabilities did the rest; William Lawson's is classified as the whisky of nightclubs and the world of the night.

Meanwhile, the company moved to Liverpool for the first time. Then he settled in Coatbridge, after Glasgow, where the blending and bottling of the whisky was carried out. To secure its malt needs, in 1972 it purchased the Macduff distillery in Banff, which also markets the malt with the name of Glen Deveron.

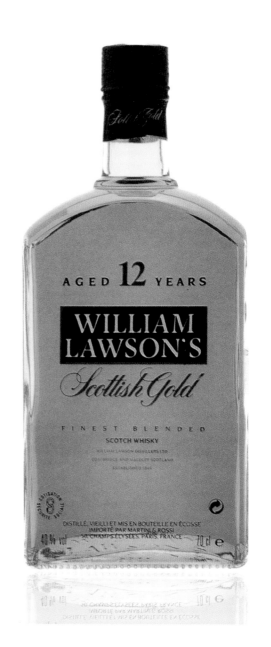

White Heather

This blend, made from Aberlour malt, is mainly distributed in France by the company Pernod-Ricard. Without being well known, it is often found in cafes and bars, where it reaches quite honorable amounts.

William Peel

The Bordeaux wine society William Pitters created this brand of blend to develop into large distributions. Experience a continuous growth. Recently, William Peel can be found also of twelve years. The brand also has ginebray bourbon (the Old Peel).

THE WHISKY LIQUORS AND THE SUCCESS OF DRAMBUIE

In the preparation of liquors based on whisky flavored with plants and sugars, honey is the most common, a tradition that goes back even to the very origins of whisky. It is explained in effect for two reasons. The brandy, uisge beatha, has medicinal origins and served to preserve plants and their healing or simply calming virtues. It has been known to harmonize very soon the whisky with the herbs of the Scottish Lands. On the other hand, the first whiskies were harsh and rough, a fine distillation was needed, and it was unlikely that consumers would have had the patience to keep it for a decade or so. Also, sweetening with honey and perfuming with the plants, a more pleasant drink was obtained. For a long time, whisky liqueurs were family or local recipes, and had never been commercialized. Unlike France or Italy, Great Britain, and especially Scotland, had almost no ancient traditions of elaborating religious liquors. And these preparations based on whisky are not rigorously liqueurs, because they did not go through distillation or prolonged maceration.

It was not until the beginning of the century that the first attempt to commercialize a whisky liqueur arose. In 1906, Malcolm MacKinnon settled in Edinburgh to enter the world of wine and spirits. He came from the Isle of Skye, where his family had for many generations a recipe with a famous origin. In effect, it was of Bonnie Prince Charles, the last of the Stuart. Since the defeat of Culloden, in 1746, he found refuge in Skye, in the home of Captain John MacKinnon, one of his most loyal officers. In gratitude, Bonnie gives him the recipe for a liquor, which many say came from France, where the prince had resided before attempting to conquer his throne. According to another version (which has nothing to do with MacKinnon's), it would be the opposite: the family had served this liquor to the prince to comfort him in his escape.

Malcolm MacKinnon applies in any case the family recipe, which he calls Drambuie, from the Gaelic expression a dram buideach, which means «the drink that satisfies». Its preparation is composed of malt and grain whiskies, heather honey and a specific liquor made from plants and herbs. The composition and proportions are evidently kept secret by the MacKinnon family. The beginning of marketing was slow, the first year were sold only twelve boxes. Because the Scots did not appreciate almost this sweetened version of their national drink. But MacKinnon was patient and stubborn. He believes in his product. The first popularization of Drambuie takes place in the dining rooms of the British Navy during the First World War.

After the death of Malcolm in 1945, his widow and the MacKinnon family would continue with the exploitation of the Drambuie, which became an important business, always independent, and the liquor was a great success in exporting. The manufacturing process was industrialized, but the recipe was, without a doubt, always the same.

Drambuie is consumed pure with ice but it is also part of numerous cocktail recipes; the aromas of whisky and heather adapt well to these preparations. The achievement of Drambuie led to the birth of other whisky liquors, none of which had the same success. For example, Dunkeld Atholl Brosse has the peculiarity of using malts that are at least twelve years old. According to a recipe that dates back to the 15th century, it included oat flakes but that is no longer the case at present. Glayva differs from the Drambuie by quite pronounced tangerine aromas. Its success in export is due to Scottish expatriates in all corners of the world. We will also mention Lochan d'Ora, made by Chivas Brothers, Sconie, a little less sugary than the others, or also Stag's Breath, in which the aromas are marked by the malts of the region and by the heather honey. As for Yachting, it is a range of liqueurs made in France after 1985 by the company Slaur. Little alcoholics, they associate the whisky with different perfumes: Passion fruit, orange, peach, coconut...

IRELAND

THE VIRTUES OF WHISKEY

To differentiate their whiskeys from the whiskeys of their Scottish cousins, the Irish bring out their precedence. According to them, the Catholic monks who evangelized the island from the fifth century created as many distilleries as monasteries, thanks to the secret that had been transmitted by the Egyptians and the Arabs. Some versions say that St. Patrick himself, the untouchable patron of the Irish nation, is the one who would have brought the techniques of making the uisge beatha or usquebaugh, this is the Gaelic version.

On the other hand, the Scots discovered the Irish liquor at the dawn of the twelfth century in a warrior run of King Henry II; they had simply imitated the Irish, without of course ever equating them, let alone overcoming them...

Historians eager for established evidence can naturally point out that no text, no trace shows this version, which seems more like a legend that has endured century after century in pubs rather than a historical reality. But why pity the Irish? They are a very friendly and welcoming people to deserve such an affront.

Whiskeys lovers, in return, should know that Irish whiskeys differ from the Scottish spirits. And, by geography or language, these two nations have found two different ways to make a brandy based on cereals. Decidedly, whiskey is a fascinating drink.

THE MASTERS DISTILLERS

In the analysis of the beginning of whiskey production, appreciable differences immediately appear. In Ireland, the peat is not used as a malting, despite being abundant on the island. The stills are certainly larger than in Scotland. In short, the triple distillation is widespread while it is exceptional for the Scots and is practiced mostly in some distilleries of the Lowlands.

But these elements do not count about the fundamental point that differentiates the Irish distilleries. Their process is completely different. Useless to look for the distribution between malts and grains, in Ireland, or the notion of blending. None of them exists and it makes no sense to rely on them to judge the quality of Irish production.

Here, everything rests on distillation. The raw material can be from non-malted barley, malt, oatmeal or rye. To extract the fifth essence, the distiller uses the two existing techniques, the *pot still* and the continuous distillation of *patent still*. The liquor goes through a triple distillation, which can combine these two techniques or use only one. Some tests are done to determine if a fourth distillation will take place...

It is useless to find a way to know the final technique used to obtain a brand or another of whiskey: it is a true state secret that few chosen ones really know. But the result is there: only in the distillery of Midleton, with the same stills are made whis-

WHISKEY AND NO WHISKY

The generalization of the term «whiskey» to designate Irish production is quite recent and has been so called to differentiate it from scotch. In the last century, for example, Watt's label, in Londonderry, bears the mention of «old Irish whisky», and is also the case for Tyrconnell. According to Michael Jackson, the term *lühiskey* is used only in Dublin, and not in other towns, such as Cork.

In Ireland, the sea is almost omnipresent and gives its soul to this country.

keys as different as Jameson, Paddy, John Power or Tullamore Dew. More importantly, we are talking about fame and well-represented brands.

Or, the immense majority of them have been elaborated in the course of the centuries in two different distilleries, or in several....

An unthinkable alchemy in Scotland.

The story explains some of these methods well. In this way, the use of non-malted barley (in a proportion that varies between 60 and 80% of the total) results from a tax on the malt introduced at the beginning of the last century, which has forced the distillers to use the «natural» barley. And it is very likely that the aggressiveness of the brandy obtained is such that a third distillation is necessary to reach a satisfactory result.

Likewise, the superior size of the Irish pot stills is also the consequence of a decision of the authorities in the 19th century. To fight the clandestine, the license was only granted to some facilities of some importance.

To be profitable, the distilleries chose to increase the volume of their stills, even

multiplying them as in Scotland. The triple distillation produces stronger spirits, up to 80% alcohol. Also, before aging, a first reduction is made with pure water, to reduce it to 63%. This fact makes the whiskey less need to age compared to the Scottish malt. Three years are the legal minimum, but the Irish distillers consider that a period of seven years is ideal. There are some older whiskeys, but they are an exception.

GREATNESS AND DECADENCE

When Aeneas Coffey fine-tuned his distilling continuous still in 1831, he was a tax man in Ireland, and it was entirely natural for him to propose it to the distillers on the island. They rejected the invention, because estimated that the liquor obtained in this way was too light in comparison with the style of their production. Well, already at the time, the power and aromatic qualities of the Irish whiskeys were appreciated, even preferred to the scotches, judged as rougher. This preference continued to develop until the beginning of the 20th century, to such an extent that whiskey became a sales leader in many markets; and first of all Great Britain! In the bars of New York, asking for a whiskey was evidently implying that one was Irish. At that time, the volumes of whiskey exported were superior to those of scotch. In Ireland there are about thirty distilleries (against a thousand at the beginning of the 19th century), but they work at full capacity.

This golden age, which the Irish still remember with great pride, fell apart in those years. The American prohibition, from 1920, brutally suppressed the most important whiskey market. The worst thing was that the American clandestine distillers baptized with the name of whiskey or Irish their infamous poison, based on alcohol of beet and bitumen, thing that harmed the reputation of the Irish production when the market reopened, years later.

Moreover, rejected the blending, the Irish were unable to fight against the economic power that empowered the Scots; their prices were much higher. In short, the agricultural crisis that shook Ireland in the early twentieth century exhausted barley resources and distillers did not have sufficient financial to enter foreign markets. And the secession of Great Britain left the country bloodless.

For some years, the distilleries closed one after the other. After the Second World War, only a handful remained. In order to react, four survivors, Jameson, Power, Cork and Tullamore, decided to unite in 1966 and to found the Irish Distillers group. They concentrated their means in a single modern distillery, in Midleton, in the south of Ireland. In 1972, they joined with Old Bushmills, located in Ulster.

In the late 1980s, a British spirits society attempt to buy them.

Unthinkable for Irish pride: the national whiskey could not pass into the hands of the hereditary enemy. Irish Distillers preferred to appeal to France, and the Pernod-Ricard group rescued it in 1987. Its commercial power proved its effectiveness and, afterwards, the sales of whiskey did not stop increasing.

In 1987 an old distillery, repurchased by an independent society, was reborn in Cooley. Its founder and president, John

THE CLANDESTINE *POTHEEN*

As in Scotland, clandestine distillation existed for a long time to not pay state taxes, lasting for many years, and some affirmed that it is not totally disappeared.

Called *potheen,* probably taken from a Gaelic deformation of the pot still, this clandestine whiskey made in the farms scattered throughout the island has nothing to do with legal production. Colorless, lacking aging and very rough, remember the pomace and other fruit alcohols produced by the distillers of wines from the French countryside. Although it is not of good quality, it has all the charm of secrecy for the Irish. For this purpose, the following anecdote is often told in Irish pubs: a tax man came to close a clandestine distillery and told his Owner: «You know why I am here, not you?». And the other replied: «Of course I know, but I am truly devastated because I cannot serve you. I have nothing currently in stock».

Teeling, became interested in the potential of Irish whiskey in 1970, when he was studying at Harvard. At some point, he was tempted to buy Irish Distillers, but eventually he created his own company with the help of Donal Kinsella, Paul Power and William McCarter. The latter, PDG of the Irish subsidiary of Fruit of the Loom, was also the owner of the old Watt distillery of Londonderry.

After renewing its distillery, this new company has put on the market, since 1992, many prestigious brands such as Tyrconnell, Kilbegaan and Locke's. It uses techniques quite different from those of Irish Distillers, such as double distillation and blending. It is also specialized in the production of specific whiskeys for large distribution companies, such as Intermarché in France or Dunnes in Ireland.

Wild and nostalgic landscape, with the typical lights of Ireland.

Bushmills

Type: **blend and whiskey malt.**
Origin: **Northern Ireland.**
Owner: **Irish Distillers.**
Date of birth: **1608.**

Having been licensed since 1608, the Old Bushmills distillery is the oldest in the world, so much so that it has practically never ceased to function. Unfortunately, the current buildings are not that old; with a violent fire in 1885 practically everything was destroyed. But the whole rebuilt today has a lot of charm, with its pagoda chimneys that remind us that malt is essential here.

The place is very important in the history of whiskey. In the north of Ireland, in the county of Antrim, the small village of Bushmills is next to the Giant's Causeway. This picturesque geological site is formed by large regular basalt slabs, which seem to be handmade. They sink into the sea in the direction of Scotland, which is a few kilometers away. An Irish legend tells: from here once an Irish giant set out, with a barrel over his shoulder, in order to make discover whiskey to the Scots...

Before its «historical» license, the Bushmills region was known to have practiced the distillation of liquor since the fifteenth century. The distillery was created by Thomas Philipps. This representative of the king in Northern Ireland had in effect the right to grant distillation licenses, which he was quick to do.

For a long time, malting has been done in situ, using a little peat, which is exceptional in Ireland. The water, taken from a stream that flows into the Bush River, is flavored by the peat bogs it crosses before reaching the Old Bushmills distillery.

The particularity of Old Bushmills is to use only malt to elaborate its different whiskeys, practicing the triple distillation. From this fact, it appears that for a long time they have only sold a single malt, called simply Bushmills Malt. Barely peaty and without trace of smoked, it is a clear and smooth whiskey, with a beautiful ex-tension at the end. Like virtually all whiskeys, it carries no mention of age.

The main brand is Bushmills, also called Old Bushmills in some presentations. It is a classic blend within the Irish style.

There is a luxury version, the Black Bush, which has a stronger proportion of malt, which is not usually mentioned on bottles.

The distillery produces Coleraine, a more confidential light blend, found mostly locally. It is named after an old distillery that ceased all activity since 1980.

Jameson

Type: **Irish whiskey.**

Origin: **Midleton.**

Owner: **Irish Distillers.**

Date of birth: **1780.**

The most distinguished of all the whiskeys is the image of its founder, John Jameson, whose aristocratic portrait adorns the bottle of twelve years of age, with the slogan *Sine metu* («Without Fear»). Today it heads the export sales lists and is very representative of the Irish style, hence the name... of a

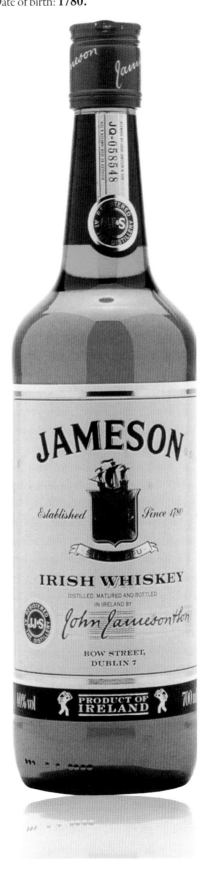

The old distillery of Midleton has been transformed into an information center about the history of whiskey.

Kilbeggan

Type: **Irish whiskey.**
Origin: **Kilbeggan.**
Owner: **Cooley Distillery.**
Date of birth: **1757.**

The small village of Kilbeggan, in the center of Ireland, houses a distillery whose first historical sign dates back to 1757. Customs records dates the production of eau-de-vie from 1762. The buildings were used for the manufacture of beers and also whiskeys and flour until the beginning of the 19th century, by the McManus, Codd and Brett families. Patrick Brett, the distiller, died in 1838 and five years later, the entire facility was sold to John Locke, a distiller who had previously worked in Tullamore. It was a small rural distillery, typical in Ireland where hundreds are counted. The grandchildren of John Locke, James Harvey and John Edward, modernized it between 1860 and 1920, benefiting from the arrival of the railroad, after a channel, to be able to stock up on raw materials and export their products. It is at this time when the Kilbeggan brand develops, notably in the export, where it knows a great success.

On the other hand, the Kilbeggan distillery would not enjoy its fate. Shaken by the closure of the American market in 1920, it never managed to rediscover satisfactory sales and ceased all activity in 1953. Then the buildings had several owners: one German dedicated in pig farming, then an engineering company installed some workshops, without success. After all, a local association was created to protect the site, which was preserved in the same way since the 19th century. In 1987, the recent Cooley Distillery society repurchased the facilities and the Kilbeggan brand. The cellars were renovated, a cooperage was created and Kilbeggan whiskey was re-launched, specifically for export.

Known also under the name of Brusna, Kilbeggan currently offers aging cellars for the different brands of Cooley society. A museum has been opened in the buildings, which receives around 30,000 visitors every year.

Scotsman, who belongs to the Haig family, the great scotch dynasty.

Arriving in Dublin in 1770, John Jameson is associated with three aristocrats who own a distillery in Bow Street, in the center of the city. He became the only owner in 1780 and completely refurbished the buildings according to his own principles. He was a perfectionist: he only used barley of excellent quality, which was distilled only in *pot stills*. He also developed aging in Sherry casks, bought by weight of gold from Spain, significantly lengthening the duration of rest. The workers in his distillery were better paid than in others and had medical services in the company; this was evidently very rare at the time, not only in Ireland. It is also said that until the end, Jameson knew the name of each of his workers, although they were more numerous than at the beginning. In addition to the notoriety of his whiskeys that not cease to develop, John Jameson was also the first of a true whiskey dynasty. Some of his sons had their own distillery and, today, their descendants hold positions of responsibility in the Irish Distillers group. The latter also establishes its position in the old distillery of Bow Street, modernized, where today is a small but very

interesting museum, the Irish Whiskey Corner. And one of the great-grandchildren of John Jameson is none other than Marconi, the inventor of the TSH.

Since entering the Irish Distillers group in 1966, John Jameson whiskeys are made in Midleton, but their specific recipe has not been modified at all. The old Midleton distillery, near Cork, has recently been converted into a museum, the Jameson Heritage Center. There is the largest still in the world, with a capacity of 143,872 liters! The standard Jameson, very popular in Dublin but also exported, is clear and smooth. There is a Jameson of twelve years, of great perfection, which is considered the best Irish whiskey by many tasters. In another time, there was a fifteen year and a twenty year in the Jameson range, but they are not very widespread in our days. The society affirms today that the Jameson does not need to wait long to reach the summum of its qualities. But you can think that so much time in stock is equally very expensive...

Equally elaborated by the company Jameson, whose name appears on the label, the Crested Ten is very light in structure, maintaining the style of the house.

Paddy

Type: **Irish whiskey.**
Origin: **Midleton.**
Owner: **Irish Distillers.**
Date of birth: **at the beginning of 1920.**

It is quite rare that a spirit bears the name of his salesman, but this is the case of Paddy. This whiskey, made by the Cork Distilleries, had a representative so active at the beginning of the century, Paddy O'Flaherty, that consumers took the habit of asking for a «Paddy» in the bars of the city. The brand was born, and developed to this day, retaining a great popularity in Cork and other Irish towns.

Second city of the republic, Cork, like its surroundings, has distilleries since the 18th century. Located to the south of the island, the port has always played an essential role in Irish economic life. There are the breweries of two brands that compete with the Guinness of Dublin, Murphy's and Beamish.

In 1867, four distilleries in the city joined a fifth, that of Midleton, to found the Cork Distilleries. Its main facility was located in Midleton, where James Murphy, the director, built the largest copper still in the world, with a capacity of 143,872 liters and which has been used until 1975. Today it can be admired at the Jameson Heritage Center, in Midleton.

Founded in 1796, the Midleton distillery benefited above all from a spring of great purity and abundance. This advantage explains why, since its creation in 1966, the Irish Distillers group has chosen this place to create a new distillery, very modern and unfortunately quite ugly, where most of its whiskeys are made. The other distilleries of Cork have disappeared with the crisis of Irish whiskey, North Mali in 1920 and Watercourse in 1975.

Paddy today is the only brand that maintains the style of Cork whiskeys, with a certain power and in the end a bit dry. It has nothing to do with the charm and elegance of the Dublin whiskeys, the Paddy is totally Irish.

In Ireland, whiskey is always consumed with a little water.

Power

Type: **Irish whiskey.**
Origin: **Midleton.**
Owner: **Irish Distillers.**
Date of birth: **1791.**

The John Power's Gold Label has long been Jameson's great rival. Both from Dublin, the two distilleries that were almost neighboring, had been created with some years of distance. James Power was the founder of John's Lane, but it is to his son John that the brand pays homage, since he made of its development in the course of the last century. Especially inventive, he was the first to put the whiskey in bottles (while they were only sold in casks), installed a steam engine and electrified his distillery. On the other hand, Power was the first packaged whiskey, the Baby Power. One of the descendants of James Power, Frank O'Reilly, was for a long-time leader of Irish Distillers. On the other hand, the distillery has been one of the last to work in Dublin, before the concentration in Midleton. Today it is occupied by the National College of Arts. Very popular in Ireland, where it is one of the best-selling brands, the Power has taken for symbol the stylized representation of three swallows, which always appear on the neck of the bottle. This whiskey, undoubtedly less elegant than its rival Jameson, has a lot of power, marked by malt, deriving from its elaboration only in *pot still.*

Tullamore Dew

Type: **Irish whiskey.**
Origin: **Midleton.**
Owner: **Iris Distillers.**
Date of birth: **1829.**

Located in the heart of Ireland, the small village of Tullamore developed a lot from the 19th century thanks to the whiskey industry. In the vicinity, a good quality barley was produced in large quantities, and, above all, the proximity of the canal along the east to the west of the island allowed rapid commercialization.

The popularity of this whiskey is due to one of its owners, Daniel E. Williams, who uses his initials, DEW, to launch his main brand, with this slogan: «Give every man his DEW». The pun is only for the Anglophones: DEW is pronounced in effect as the English word meaning «due»... A typical example of Irish humor. Another example of humor, this time reported by Michael Jackson: according to this whiskey specialist, the Tullamore owes its success in France to the fact that it is pronounced «tout l'amour»... The brand was then reacquired by the Irish Distillers group, and it is one of the lightest whiskeys in Ireland, but with a great aromatic finesse. It is also marketed in a high range version packed in a cooked earth jar, with the Gaelic mention *uisge beatha*.

The distillery stopped working since the 1950s, but the Williams company continues to produce Irish Mist whiskey liqueur.

Tyrconnell

Type: **Irish whiskey.**
Origin: **Riverstown.**
Owner: **Cooley Distillery.**
Date of birth: **1876.**

The John Locke distillery between the two wars.

If a whiskey symbolizes all the affection Ireland has for horses, this is Tyrconnell. Because it is the name of a racehorse that, in 1876, Queen Victoria won while she was quoted at one hundred against one. With such success, its owner, Andrew A. Watt, decided to give this name to his main brand of whiskey, which was made in Londonderry. Tyrconnell is also the name of an old manor in northwest Ireland, owned by the O'Donnell family.

The company dates back to 1762 (date that appears today on the label of Tyrconnell) but was at the time a business of wines and spirits, including wholesale grocer's shop. His first steps in distillation go back to 1830, when he teamed up with Ross T. Smyth, owner of a distillery located on Abbey Street. In 1854, the union takes the name of A.A. Watt & Co., having as president David Watt. This is the golden age of Irish whiskey and Watt takes full advantage of it: in 1887, his Abbey Street distillery is one of the most important in Ireland, with a production that passes 9 million liters. With Inishowen, Tyrconnell is the best-known brand, especially in the United States: film of baseball games at Yankee Stadium proves its presence in advertising panels.

At the beginning of the century, Watt is associated with two other distilleries in Northern Ireland, Avoniel and Connswater, to form United Distillers Company, the largest producer in Ulster. Naturally, after the creation of the Republic of Ireland, it was associated with the DCL of Scotland. But the closing of the American market proved fatal to it. The group is repurchased by the Scots in 1922 and the Watt distillery closes in 1925. The Tyrconnel brand would disappear a few years later. His former leaders wanted to create a new society, Iriscot, which did not distill itself, but imported Scotch grains mixed with other spirits under the Watt brands. After a fire, which led to the destruction of its facilities, the company was definitively closed in 1970.

After the creation in 1987 of the company Cooley Distillery, one of the partners, William McCarter, contributed the assets of Andrew A. Watt, and essentially the Tyrconnell brand. Production began in 1989, and the first cask was bottled in July 1992 by Patricia Morgan, a descendant of John Locke. The commercialization of Tyrconnel began less than a year later.

Qualified as *pure pot still single malt whiskey*, Tyrconnell was the result of a double distillation carried out in *pot still*. Its malted character and its softness differentiated it widely from the rest of the Irish production.

AND ALSO...

Avoca
This brand was launched at the end of 1994 by Cooley Distillery. Distributed exclusively for the chain of Dunnes stores in Ireland.

Connemara
Taking the name of the most romantic region of Ireland, this «single malt» of Cooley Distillery has the distinction of being cleanly peaty.

Dunphy's
This light whiskey from Irish Distillers is quite rare. It exists under two different presentations, for export and for the internal market.

Hewitts
Bearing the name of an old Cork distillery, which made a grain whiskey, this fairly light Irish Distillers whiskey looks like a blend.

Inishowen
This new brand launched by Cooley Distillery is a smooth blend. It is named af-

ter the northernmost peninsula of Ireland, kept for many centuries by the fortress of Burt Castle, belonging to the clan of O'Doherty. In this region, the distillation is ancient.

Locke's

Launched in Ireland as a strongly malted upper blend, this brand of Cooley Distillery is named after James and John Locke, old owners of the Kilbeggan distillery (see this brand). The last years of this society were marked by a resounding scandal. When Locke wanted to take control of a foreign group, the rumors of corruption of ministers come out, without the justice could prove anything. Then, allegations of fraud about raw materials and illicit whiskey shipments through an underground pipeline were launched. Scratched by the debts and seeing that its sales decreased, the Locke company stopped distilling in 1953 and closed definitively in 1963.

Midleton

The Distillery of Midleton belonging to

Irish Distillers produces the Midleton Very Rare, in very limited quantities (each bottle was numbered). This release from the search results for the distillery of new aging methods.

Murphy's

This old Cork distillery has the same name as the famous beer of the same city. Today it is a blend elaborated in Midleton by Irish Distillers.

O'Hara

This brand of blend of Cooley Distillery is reserved for the chain of Intermarché stores. It is currently available in France, and, depending on the results, the distribution group does not rule out proposing it in other European countries where it is introduced.

Redbreast

This twelve-year-old is a blend from Jameson malts, but bottled and distributed by another company, the Gilbey's Irish subsidiary.

In pubs, whiskey is matched with beer.

THE WHISKEY LIQUORS

As in Scotland, the Irish distillers have a great experience in making liqueurs and other preparations based on whiskey. The best known is of course Baileys, launched in 1974 by IDV (Grand Metropolitan). Its creators have managed to stabilize the mixture of the cream with alcohol. With 17% alcohol, Baileys knows a great commercial success around the world. On the other hand, the initial intention was to bottle the famous cocktail, irish coffee, but the result is far away, the taste of coffee has been replaced by a caramelized chocolate.

Pubs painted in bright colors are part of the Irish national heritage, with the same right as whiskeys.

The success of Baileys has led to the appearance of many rival products, manufactured by both distilleries and dairy companies: O'Darby, Carolans, Waterford Cream, etc., but with less success than Baileys, which benefits from the advantage to have been the first in the market. Thanks to intelligent advertising campaigns, Baileys has certainly contributed to the international popularity of Ireland and its whiskeys.

There are other types of whiskey-based liquors, which do not use cream, but are less sold. Irish Distillers also makes a punch ready for use called Snug, based on whiskey, sugar, lemon and spice cloves, to which it is sufficient to add boiling water.

AMERICA

FROM PIONEERS TO INDUSTRIALISTS

The conquest of the New World offered virgin lands to the old Europe, and people rushed there from the 18th century. Scottish and Irish were part of the expedition and, with them, the taste of whiskey of which they possessed the secret of the production. On the other hand, crossing the Atlantic generated surprising paradoxes in the matter of distillation and consumption of «fire water», as the Indians, the first occupants of the American continent, called it.

On the one hand, the American distillers forgot the Scottish or Irish methods to develop new ones, using other raw materials and elaborate very different spirits. On the other hand, while the United States was the first world market for whiskey, its production was much lower than its consumption. Therefore generally very proud of everything that is *made in USA*, the Americans despised instead their bourbons and other whiskeys for the Canadian scotch and whiskey. And there are almost no more examples in history (apart from the religious prohibition of Muslim countries) of an anti-alcohol hysteria comparable to that which provoked the thirteen years of prohibition.

DEEP DOWN IN THE UNITED STATES

The small town of Lynchburg, in Tennessee, and its 360 inhabitants are a portrait that can suggest the real age of American whisky (or rather whiskey). Because this is where Jack Daniel's, one of the first brands in quality and volume, is made after more than a century. Manifestly, the town has not changed almost since then, and its appearance reflects the extent to which whiskey is first and foremost a rural product, born from the depths of the country, and has nothing to do with the dynamism and gigantism of the rest of the country. But, in this privileged place of whiskey, it is forbidden to buy or drink alcohol. It is an unimaginable situation in Scotland, Champagne or Bordeaux. It is made with methods that do not owe anything to Scotland, although Jack Daniel was of British origin, among other things the filtration on wood charcoal of the distilled liquor. This long and expensive technique, but of a real effectiveness to remove its impurities, had never been considered in the ancestral territories of whiskey.

It is not an isolated case, and outside of some exceptions nearby (in Indiana especially), it is not in the United States where it is necessary to look for large industrial premises that produce grain whiskeys as in Scotland or Canada. The essence of American production is in effect in the agricultural states of Kentucky and Tennessee, since Virginia or Maryland play a complementary role. And it is symptomatic that there is no distillery on the east and west coasts or in the south. A somewhat surprising paradox if you compare this situation with that of beer, also coming from Europe and established throughout the country. If the official story has long given the name of Pastor Elijah, or Elias, Craig, as the first American distiller in 1789, it seems that we must go back before. The colonization of Kentucky began fifteen years earlier, and the distillery Evan Williams, in Louisville, claimed its foundation in 1783.

Beyond this mess of data, one cannot imagine the first pioneers, according to their progression towards the west, depending on the external supply for the consumption of whiskey. There must have been some Scots among them who knew the techniques clandestinely used in the Highlands.

On the other hand, the authorities encouraged the distillation. In this way, Thomas Jefferson, governor of Virginia, offers lots of 15 hectares of land in Kentucky to anyone who settled there and grew corn. Such surface produces too much to feed a single family, and the means of transport are insufficient at the time to be able to market the surplus. The distillation of whiskey solves the problem, also representing a financial contribution.

As in Scotland, the distillation quickly interests the government and the first rate is voted on in 1791, only eight years after Independence. It is true that the young country needs money...

Despite their European origins, American distillers quickly acclimatize to new conditions. Very soon, corn, rye, even wheat is preferred to malted barley, that is truly long and expensive to produce. In the same way, as it was known, continuous distillation was preferred to the traditional still, even for its speed.

Another innovation, the burning of new barrels. The technique is not entirely new: it probably dates back to the origins of the first spirits (Armagnac and cognac), because it eliminates the tannins in the wood, shortening the duration of aging. But if in Scotland it was not almost used, in the United States it was a true believe. Because it was vital to go fast, consumers did not wait and quality demands began to arrive. These are undoubtedly also the same reasons that lead to the development of filtration on wood charcoal, before aging as in Tennessee, or before in other regions.

THE CONFLICT OF PROHITION

At the end of the 19th century, everything seems to be in place for a real boom in the whiskey industry: abundant resources in cereals and water, a very specific style, financial means. There were some scandals that come to the fore as the fraud of quality or financial understandings between producers; Scotland has also had similar experiences. In 1909, under pressure from producers, the federal government promulgates the definition of large categories of whiskeys and their methods of production.

However, a serious danger threatens production. As in other countries (France or Britain also knew abolitionists at the same time), a powerful movement is formed against alcohol in general and whiskey in particular, bringing together women and doctors... and xenophobes. Indeed, the trade of alcohol and beer is often in this period of German origin.

Since 1881, Kansas had banned the manufacture and consumption of alcohol, followed by Georgia in 1907. The First World War precipitated the movement: beer and whiskey take advantage of the Germans, weaken the troops, deprive the European allies of grain and bringing syphilis. After two attempts in 1917 and 1919, the eighteenth amendment prohibiting the production, distribution and consumption of alcohol throughout the United States is voted on January 16, 1920.

The effects are catastrophic, and in the first place for whiskey producers. They are forced to close or, desperately, become distillers of «medicinal» alcohol. But the ravages are not only limited to distilleries.

THE ORIGINS OF BOURBON

The most famous American whiskey owes its name to a small Kentucky county. It bears this name in tribute to the support provided by the French royal family to the Americans in their War of Independence against Great Britain. The distillation started in Kentucky, but today, that county has not produced a single drop of bourbon for a long time.

Most Americans, in fact, do not want to stop drinking alcohol altogether. On the contrary, the attractiveness of prohibition naturally excites its consumption. The underground is developed from the vote of the amendment: unofficial bars, the *speakeasies*, will be opened everywhere, and contraband is developed on a large scale.

Everyone is involved: the New York taxis that come and go from Canada to buy whiskey that they then sell eight times more expensive; shippers of all kinds, and even submarines, which transport scotch bought in the Bahamas or Cuba and land it on American shores, sometimes in floating containers or torpedoes. Above all, a large clandestine industry will emerge. The stills are counted by hundreds of thousands. Two liters of potato alcohol, 12 centiliters of potassium acetate, 1.5 milliliters of copper sulphuthium, 1.5 milliliters of alkali, 3 centiliters of manganese oxide and 25 centiliters of diluted Javel water, probably the most frightening of migraines, even worse. The bottles are hidden in the coats or even in the women's skirts, alcohol is hidden in the most recondite places: cisterns, cash registers, etc. Tourism develops at a huge pace towards Canada or Cuba, which became a world center for the cocktail.

Besides the folklore, the prohibition allows the mafia to develop a power that will not stop growing. Contraband, clandestine distillations, traffic of all kinds bring many dollars, generating struggles that grow between different bands that plague cities like Chicago.

The failure of the abolitionists is total, and the great recession that began in 1929 put everyone in agreement. The Democrat Franklin Roosevelt, who campaigned for the suppression of the ban, is elected in 1932, and kept his word since 1933.

The American whiskey industry was never again what it was. Meanwhile, the Canadians and the Scots took advantage of the situation: they had the necessary stocks to flood the American market with their whiskeys. On the other hand, they produce elegant and lighter products that make bourbon a rough and rude product.

The turkey has become the official emblem of the United States.

THE WHISKEY VOCABULARY

Using specific methods and products, American whiskey has generated its own terms.

— The **bourbon** must contain at least 51% corn and be distilled exclusively in Kentucky.

— The mention «Bottled in bond» gives the legal guarantee that the whiskey comes from a single and unique distillery, which has aged in deposits controlled by the State and that has been bottled in the same place. The presence of a fiscal seal on the cap is a guarantee of quality for the buyer.

— The **corn whiskey** contains at least 80% corn. It is a product of local consumption, without large brands spread.

— The **light whiskey** is distilled between 80 and 85 degrees of alcohol. It can be similar to a straight whiskey.

— The **rye whiskey** contains at least 51% rye.

— «Sour mash» means a specific manufacturing mode used by most whiskey distillers, and especially bourbon distillers. To reinforce the aromas, the residue of the preceding distillation can be added during the cooking of the cereals, during the fermentation, during the yeast, or even in all the phases. The term sour, may be poorly perceived by consumers, this mention has been omitted for a long time by distillers, but begins to be considered a sign of quality.

—The **straight whiskey** comes from a single distillery, even from a single distillation, with a percentage of alcohol lower than 80 degrees. Like the «single malt», almost always elaborated in continuous distillation, the straight whiskeys represent the aristocracy. If there are many together, this gives **a blended straight whiskey**. And if the distiller adds neutral alcohol again, you get a **blended whiskey**.

After the Second World War, the whiskey will find the place it deserved. Bourbon will be the main beneficiary, with Tennessee whiskey.

Made with rye, the most authentic of the whiskeys, did not stop declining, because its bitter taste did not play in his favor. Only a few distillers still make it today.

THE CANADIAN PARADOX

If Canada has now become one of the most important producers of whiskeys in the world, this is undoubtedly not due to the will of the political powers, or even to a majority of the population. Of course, in this large, sparsely populated country with a rough climate, whiskey has been appreciated since the beginning of colonization, and small distilleries have proliferated very fast. But Puritan morality, Protestant or Catholic on the other hand, quickly tried to limit expansion, even to prohibit consumption.

Today still, there are severe restrictions, which vary from one province to another, affect the places of consumption, not to mention advertising for alcoholic beverages.

This abolitionist attitude is illustrated by the following anecdote, told by Tilomas Dewar, of the Scottish society with the same name, and reacquired by James Darwen in his recent work *la Grande Histoire du whisky.*

«During the 1920s, at the time I visited a country of prohibition, Canada, I tried to get some whiskey next to a train driver, but without success. He advises me nothing less to try it in a warehouse at the next stop.

–They sell whiskey, I asked.

–Are you sick, sir, or do you have a doctor's certificate?

–No.

–Then I cannot serve you, I believe that our mixture against cholera would suit you. Taste a bottle. Incredible, I was very surprise, receive a bottle of familiar form that carried on one side a label that said «Mix against anger, drink a glass of wine every two hours until necessary» and on the other side the label from a well-known brand of Scotch whiskey that modesty prevents me from quoting».

The placing in barrels of American bourbon.

This non-generalized prohibition does not prevent distillers from developing. It is even less pressing, in the image of the American Hiram Walker who will be established in 1858 to create his first distillery. He considers the conditions of work too hard in the United States for this activity, although its main market is constituted by its country of origin. It is no coincidence that most of the Canadian distilleries are located today in Ontario and Quebec, very close to the border with the United States. Moreover, here are sources of supply in raw materials such as the main urban concentrations, but the sign of the true Canadian whiskey market is located in the south, on the other side of the border.

Just as they build the most powerful cars that can only drive at ridiculously low speeds, Americans love whiskey but were able to generalize the ban across the country, causing the interruption of their own production.

This period represents an unparalleled great fortune for Canadian whiskey. The country was about to generalize abstinence, but the United States was the first to take this path. But suddenly, Canada no longer had to close its distilleries, which retained the right to produce for export, in order to take advantage of this unexpected wealth.

The companies Seagram and Hiram Walker amassed their fortune, to the point of being today the world leaders in the distillation and distribution of whiskey (Scottish, Canadian or American), but also of other spirits.

This prosperity is nothing more than a stroke of luck or the chance of history. Since the Canadian distillers have also

The distillery of the Canadian Club of Walkerville, at the beginning of the century and nowadays.

known how to innovate in the matter of whiskey. The essential merit is of Hiram Walker, the creator of the Canadian Club brand. When he created his distillery in Walkerville, Ontario, he significantly innovated the social plan, but above all he started up a new type of whiskey. Using a lot of rye, malted or not malted, but also other cereals, its blend mixes high quality whiskeys, thanks to a choice of high quality raw materials and a distillation of great purity, with alcohols practically neutral in flavor and aroma. The result gives a whiskey marked in flavor, but with a lightness

and an absence of aggressiveness. It is often described as «rye whisky», but this name should not deceive the amateur, nor above all create confusion with the American «rye». Well, in Canada, rye is always associated with other whiskeys and especially with a very purified grain alcohol, which is not the case in the United States.

All the genius of Hiram Walker is here: to preserve the aromatic qualities of different basic cereals, thus being able to seduce many consumers. The success would be quick with this key and most other distillers followed his example, creating in this way a

Canadian style at once light and sweet but aromatic, capable of seducing a large clientele in many countries.

More than the Scots or the Irish, the Canadians revealed themselves as the fearsome blenders. In this way, Samuel Bronfman, who made Seagram a successful phenomenon, was always passionate about the development of new recipes. When he created the Crown Royal, he had to try over six hundred compositions before finding one that was to his liking. It is true that he tries celebrating the visit to Canada of King George VI...

Ancient Age

Type: **bourbon.**
Origin: **Frankfort (Kentucky).**
Owner: **Ancient Age Distilling.**
Date of birth: **1869.**

With its initials AA, even AAA (for ten years), the Ancient Age is a classic bourbon well known and appreciated in the United States. Its distillery was created in Frankfurt in 1869. The town, which on the other hand is the capital of the State, although being ten times less important than Louisville, does not owe its name to the German city, but possibly to the first pioneers who came and went established, the Frank family, no doubt at the end of the eighteenth century.

The region is one of the first to have whiskey, and the old qualifier is used for many brands. Ancient Age is a milestone in this tradition and claims the use of good old recipes from another time. The company has changed owners many times and belonged to the Schenley group for a while. But, since 1982, it was resold to a group of partners who were interested in the spirits sector.

The buildings have not been barely changed after a long time and certainly present a historical character. There is a large warehouse, which was built in 1953, when the distillery exceeded the 2 million hectoliters produced at the time of the ban. Then, the 5 million hectoliters have been widely exceeded... A pavilion in the traditional style dating from 1930 now houses visitors.

Without bringing any indication of aging, the Ancient Age is bottled at 86 degrees proof (around 43% alcohol), this is enough for a bourbon. It brings more lightness and is ideal for the appetizer. The Ancient Ancient Age (AAA) knows an aging of ten years, and this time earns it much naturalness and aromatic expressions. It is very appreciated, especially by the bartenders. There is also another version of Ancient Age under the name of Leestown, available in certain regions only. This is the name of the first hamlet, dated 1773, which gave birth to the people of Frankfort.

Black Velvet

Type: **Canadian blend.**
Origin: **Lethbridge (Alberta).**
Owner: **IDV (Grand Metropolitan).**
Date of birth: **1951.**

In 1933, Gilbey, a great gin specialist in London, settled in Canada and created a first distillery in the vicinity of Toronto. After the Second World War, the company launches a Canadian whiskey in order to take advantage of the great resources of the country's cereals.

Jack Napier, the master distiller, makes the Black Velvet from 1951. It is currently distilled and brewed at the Palliser distillery in Lethbridge, Alberta. Consistent with the traditional techniques of Canadian whiskey, it is distilled in two stages: a first brandy born from a mixture of rye, barley and malt aged for two years in small oak barrel. After that is mixed with more neutral grain (corn) brandy before aging for four years in burned barrels. That technique of *blending at birth,* the mix at the beginning, according to the people in charge of Gilbey, give softness and a dissolution in the Black Velvet.

When bottled, the reduction of the alcohol grain is carried out with a water filtered over carbon and demineralized. When the first bottles of Black Velvet were shipped to the Manitoba liquor store, the first customer demanded that each bottle be packed separately, and not in boxes as the manufacturer had intended. This requirement caught them off guard since they did not have rectangular boxes yet, but Gilbey accepts the proposal of a supplier who proposes to use simple brown cardboard tubes. The result was very successful, and the company has remained faithful to the tube to pack their bottles. In Canada, it was only consumed at the end of the year parties, but it was exported a lot. The Black Velvet has the vocation of an international whiskey and is currently distributed in sixty countries. Since 1969, its promotion was secured by advertising with the ad «Black Velvet Lady», a superb mannequin usually blonde, dressed in black and long elegant clothes. This mannequin changed every year.

The softness of the Black Velvet is appreciated natural, but Gilbey also develops its consumption in very varied cocktails.

The Black Velvet is the most sold of the whiskeys made by society, but the range is extended to other varieties using the term *velvet* associated with other adjectives: Red Velvet is a superior whiskey, which is aged for more time, destined mainly to Japan; the Regal Velvet is its equivalent for the American market. There is also a Royal Velvet and a Golden Velvet.

Blanton's

Type: **bourbon.**
Origin: **Frankfort (Kentucky).**
Owner: **Blanton Distilling.**
Date of birth: **1895.**

This small distillery is about a century old and was created by Colonel Albert J. Blanton. It has the distinction of marketing its bourbon in an original way in relation to most American distillers. It does not practice any mixture or union between the barrels of its production, and each of them has a specific container. Each label bears the handwritten mention, specifying the date of bottling, the degree of alcohol and even the cellar and storage box numbers of each barrel.

The durability of aging and the degree of alcohol can vary, the distiller does not prepare a barrel until he considers that it has reached its fullness.

This method evidently produces very original bourbons, but of a variable quality from one barrel to another. The Blanton's Single Barrel is also packaged in a very original bottle. Its cap ends with a metal figure representing a rider, and is packed in a small velvet bag. A luxury presentation for an exceptional bourbon.

The Black Velvet bottling chain.

Canadian Club

Type: **canadian blend.**
Origin: **Walkerville (Ontario).**
Owner: **Hiram Walker (Allied Domecq).**
Date of birth: **1884.**

The Canadian Club has been created and developed by Hiram Walker, a man who made himself, that is, a person who represents the American myth. Of modest origin, he was born in 1816 in the United States, on a farm in East Douglas (Massachusetts). Ambitious, he left at twenty to work in Boston, then two years later to Detroit, in that period in full economic boom. He learned the trade in stores, then opened his own store before becoming a grain seller.

At forty, he had accumulated a capital of $40,000, which he wanted to invest in the milling and distillation. But the American environment was not convenient, especially with the hostile Michigan alcohol laws. For that reason, it crossed the river and settled right in front of Detroit, in Canadian territory, in the exact place where, in 1812, in the Second War of Independence, the Americans had wanted to disembark to free the Canadians from the British tutelage. He created a mill and a distillery from 1858. His whiskey is original for the time and is very different from American production. After searching for a long time, Hiram Walker finds a lighter, less harsh brandy, thanks to a longer distillation. It has less need to age to improve, having a lot of aroma. The Canadian style has been born, and owes everything to the inventor of the Canadian Club. Originally, it is simply called «Club Whisky», which was appreciated in the bars and clubs where businessmen and important people of the region met. In the United States it has an overwhelming success, so much that American distillers are disturbed by this rivalry and demand a law obliging Hiram Walker to clearly specify the Canadian origin of his production, because they find it too different from bourbon and other whiskeys.

The Canadian Club brand appears in 1884, but this new name does not change anything in the success of whiskey. In addition, Hiram

Walker is the first to have the idea of bottling the whiskey with his brand, then began to market it in clay pots. He was imitated by all Canadian distillers, became the number one in the country and had great success. This involves the multiplication of counterfeits (more than forty in 1900 emerge). The reaction of Hiram Walker will be up to this character: he spreads in an unprecedented campaign the names and addresses of the imitators, and among them was Charles Klyman, retailer of Chicago, forcing him to publish in the press an article entitled «A confession», where he acknowledges having sold under the brand name Canadian Club some whiskeys of a much lower quality.

Meanwhile, the mill-distillery of Hiram Walker gave birth to a true village, Walkerville, where its workers and members of the leading staff are housed. He installs public lighting, running water, and finances schools, churches, firefighters and even police. In 1885, he created a railway line, and the dynamism of Walkerville attracted many other societies of all kinds. It became officially a commune in 1890 and was united in 1935 with the neighboring town of Windsor.

He died in 1899, and his sons take over; then twenty years later his grandchildren. But finally they wanted to sell the company and found a buyer in 1926 in the person of Harry C. Hatch, a businessman and owner of Gooderham&Worts, the oldest distillery in Canada, located in Toronto. From this merger, one of the most important of the time, a group with international ambitions was born, having as a leading brand the Canadian Club. Starting in 1930, the group moved to Scotland, bought the brand Ballantine's and many other distilleries, creating the huge Dumbarton complex.

In 1987, Hiram Walker was bought by a large British group, Allied Lyons, having multiple interests in agri-food. Its division of spirits, which always bears the name of Hiram Walker, has a wide catalog of international brands, where Canadian Club is one of the stars. It was later associated with the Spanish group Domecq.

The standard version of the Canadian Club, which experiences a minimum aging of six years, has seen its presentation renewed in 1992, putting the date of foundation of the distillery, 1858. There is also a version of twelve years, the Canadian Club Classic, thought mainly for the duty-free market. The twenty-year-old enjoys a rather luxurious presentation in a decanter representing a typical mountainous landscape of Canada, with a stopper adorned with a plate in 18-carat gold. A product specifically destined for the Far East markets.

One of the distilleries where the Canadian Club is made.

Canadian Mist

Type: **Canadian blend.**
Origin: **Collingwood (Ontario).**
Owner: **Brown Forman.**
Date of birth: **1890.**

This Canadian whiskey, classic in its preparation, belongs to an American company, Brown Forman, which also owns Old Forester and Jack Daniel's. The Canadian Mist is distributed in Canada by the company Canadian Company, which has the distinction of selling the whiskeys of many societies. In addition, it has a distillery near Toronto, but only to produce wine or fruit spirits. Quite light in aromas and on the palate, the Canadian Mist is made from malted barley, corn, wheat and rye. Experience a three-year aging in oak barrels before bottling, which takes place in Kentucky. It arrival in Europe in 1993.

Crown Royal

Type: **Canadian luxury blend.**
Origin: **Waterloo (Ontario).**
Owner: **Seagram.**
Date of birth: **1939.**

They created this luxury blend, composed of more than forty whiskeys between ten and thirty years, after having tried more than six hundred different compositions. The bottle is unique in its kind, with faces carved like a diamond. Sold in an embroidered

velvet sleeve. Despite - or because of? - this luxurious character, the Crown Royal has a real commercial success for the Seagram group, with around 25 million bottles sold in the world.

It is a strong whiskey, with rich aromas marked by prolonged aging in barrels.

Four Roses

Type: **bourbon.**
Origin: **Lawrenceburg (Kentucky).**
Owner: **Seagram.**
Date of birth: **1888.**

Paradoxically, one of the best-selling bourbons in Europe, which also records excellent results in the Far East, is totally unknown in the United States, where it is not for sale.

The origin of the brand is not known and differs according to the different qualities of bourbon. One of the versions refers to the four daughters of Colonel Rose, one of the old owners of the distillery. Around 1880, a dance took place on the property, so the damsels wore all black clothes, very fashionable at the time; the colonel enhanced their elegance by giving everyone a freshly cut rose from the garden. This inspired his wife to say: « Why not give the name of «Four Roses» to your bourbon?»

This story may be too pretty, on the other hand it has been told by a descendant of the family. In Colonel Rose's house there were not four daughters but five, and above all, a gentleman like him would never have given the name of his daughters to an alcohol, even if it is very good.

According to other sayings, the name derives from the existence of four men in the family (the uncle, the father and the two children), while some also point to the fact that the Rose company owned four different production sites.

Another version tells that it was a beautiful young woman who took a day four red roses to respond favorably to the marriage

request of a certain Paul Jones. This legend approaches the historical truth, because it was Paul Jones who originally develops the brand.

At first, there was a distillery in Lawrenceburg, founded in 1818 by an Irishman, Old Joe Peyton, at the mouth of the Salt River, at Gilbert's Creek. His bourbon brand, Old Joe, was one of the oldest in Kentucky. But the old distillery no longer exists in our days, after having changed owners on numerous occasions.

Trained in the whiskey business in Georgia, Paul Jones came to Kentucky in 1886 and bought the Four Roses brand two years later from the Rose family, which operated in Tennessee. He developed it with some success, before merging in 1902 with many other distilleries to finally form Frankfort Distilleries.

His grandson, Lawrence Jones, would secure the address, especially during the ban, after having obtained authorization to produce a whiskey «for medical use». In 1910 a new distillery was built, with a Hispanic style, very surprising in Kentucky.

In 1943, the group bought Seagram, which made experience the Four Roses brand its true development from this period.

The place of Lawrenceburg has changed a lot since then. In this way, the distillery was surrounded by aging warehouses, which were rented to Wild Turkey, the rival in Lawrenceburg. After the distillation, Four Roses bourbons are shipped 80 kilometers away to Cox's Creek. They remain in the cellars in a single level, avoiding in this way the qualitative variations between different stages usually found by the producers of liquor. The Four Roses trip does not end here, since once the aging process is over, the barrels are shipped... to Scotland, for bottling and commercialization. This explains the absence of bottles of Four Rouses in the American territory. The Four Rouses brand has many different types of bourbons, and even a bourbon blend, depending on the markets to which it is destined.

The Yellow Label is the most expanded variety, especially in Europe. It is a five year, with a proportion of at least 50% of corn and bottled at 40 or 43% alcohol according to the markets.

The Black Label, also called Fine Old and that uses a different yeast, experiences an aging of six years. It is not sold in Europe.

The Super Premium, marketed mainly in Japan, contains a strong proportion of corn (60%) and experiences an aging of eight years.

Finally, the Single Barrel, which is much rarer, comes as its name indicates, from a single barrel, without blends and has 43% alcohol at the time of bottling.

I. W. Harper

Type: **bourbon.**
Origin: **Louisville (Kentucky).**
Owner: **Seagram.**
Date of birth: **1872.**

Nobody knows exactly today because Isaac Wolfe Bernheim decided to call his bourbon «I.W. Harper». Some think they are the initials of his name and he wanted to create a brand that «sounds American». Harper comes from the name of a Virginia ferry. What is certain is that the history of this brand symbolizes an entire era, that of European immigration to the United States.

A native of German Switzerland, Bernheim arrived in the United States in 1867. He started as a street vendor and begin a business in 1872 in Kentucky, with his brother Bernard. They at that time only had a bourbon barrel and $ 1,200 saved.

After a first implantation in Paducah, the Bernheim brothers moved to Louisville, the largest town in Kentucky. Their bourbon was quickly appreciated and would be one of the first to be sold bottled in this region, and Bernheim explains that «transparent glass gives whiskey a shine never seen before». The current bottle, with faces carved like a precious stone, perpetuates this tradition.

The I.W. Harper won numerous rewards in the contests, especially many gold medals, to such an extent that Bernheim will make his publicity with the following slogan: «The whiskey that won gold medals when you were still children».

The Bernheim brothers were so proud of their success in the United States that they made multiple donations in their region. In addition to bronze sculptures and the expansion of the Louisville hospital, Isaac bequeathed on his death, in 1945, a forest of more than 5,000 hectares in the vicinity of Louisville, which became a natural park receiving more than 500,000 visitors each year, with numerous species of protected trees and wild animals. There is even an old still from when the clandestine distillation was done. The distillery was acquired in the 30s by the Schenley group and currently belongs to the British group United Distillers. During the ban, he was able to continue producing a bourbon qualified as «medical». After the Second World War, the bourbon I.W. Harper was the first to be exported to Britain. Exported to more than one hundred and ten countries, it is one of the best-selling bourbons in Japan.

In a very classic style, the I.W. Harper is a very nice bourbon. It benefits from its fermentation and its aging cellars made with brick that conserve constant temperature and humidity throughout the year. There are different qualities, the variations concern the degree of alcohol but also aging, which highlights a four and a ten year.

Jack Daniels

Type: **Tennessee whiskey.**
Origin: **Lynchburg.**
Owner: **Brown Forman.**
Date of birth: **1866.**

Born in 1849, Jasper Newton Daniel, nicknamed «Jack» very soon, was the youngest of a large family, ten children, who had settled in Franklin County, Tennessee. He lost his mother very soon and his father remarried. Jack leaves quickly from the family home. From the age of seven, he worked with Dan Cali, a preacher who is also a whiskey distiller, who sold in his store. He was very interested in the techniques of distillation, to such an extent that Cali admitted him as a partner. Later, when he decided to leave the business to fully exercise his ministry, he sold it to Jack, who was only thirteen years old.

Looking to improve the quality of his whiskey, Jack Daniel began to look for an abundant source of water that was calcareous and not ferruginous. He discovered it near the town of Lynchburg, at the bottom of a cave where the water flows at a constant temperature of 13°C.

In addition to this water and the process of a sour mash fermentation, Jack Daniel's whiskey has as its originality a specific filtration process. The distilled liquor is poured into a large amount of maple wood charcoal. It melts slowly, it can take between three and eight days, before being passed to barrels of burned oak. The aging, variable, can last from four to six years.

The name of the inventor of this process, called charcoal mellowing, is unknown, but he came from Lincoln County, also in Tennessee. As a result, the young brandy is removed from its esters to bring new aromas. Although it is not noticed in the tasting, this technique contributes without any doubt to give its characteristic style to whiskey. With the indication «No. 7» (Jack never explained why he chose this figure, which can be a fetish), Jack Daniel's immediately had a real success in Tennessee. After the Civil War, the government set in motion a policy of regulation, and therefore of pricing, on distillation. In 1866. Jack Daniel took out the license, which is the first granted in the United States. His whiskey wins medals in official competitions.

Single and childless, Jack thought of his succession and formed his favorite nephew, Lem Motlow, for the management of his company. He was entrusted with it in 1907, since his health began to deteriorate: one day, he was very angry, and he violently tapped his foot in the safe of his office. At first, he suffers only from a simple limp, but his condition worsens and, in the end, he passes away in 1911.

Lem Motlow would continue with the work of Jack Daniel without changing his methods. During the prohibition, he stopped the manufacture (to retake it in 1938), meanwhile it was dedicated to the breeding and the business of mules. In 1942, there is a new stop due to cereal restrictions due to the war. He waited until 1947 to resume the activity, being sure of having the quality of cereals he wanted.

Shortly after, Lem Motlow died, but his four children named Reagor, Robert, Daniel and Connor succeeded him and remained faithful to the great principles of the founder with this slogan: «Every day we can do it, we will do our best».

Little sensitive to progress, the Motlows were nicknamed «brothers in shirtsleeves», with calm manners and far from the fashion of big cities. In the 1950s, the growth of rates and laws on transmission made their undivided financial structure unsustainable, and the Motlow brothers preferred to sell the company to the Brown Forman society of Louisville, although they continued to work.

The town of Lynchburg has not changed almost since the time of Jack Daniel, and life continues at the same pace. This permanence attracts many tourists, more than 300,000 per year. They come mainly to visit the distillery and assist in the manufacture of charcoal, which is a real show that takes place once or twice a week. With maples that are brought from the heights of Tennessee and that are dried for a year, some sawed logs that later are piled up in coal bunkers, the *ricks*. They burn outdoors and then transform into charcoal. The operation is delicate since, to obtain the coal, it is necessary to irrigate the firewood at regular intervals. This is done by experienced workers, called rickers, who are responsible of it. Finely grinded, the charcoal is then put into large vats many meters high to filter the brandy.

This specific process was finally recognized by the American authorities, who created in 1941 the category of «Tennessee whiskey» for whiskey made in this way.

The most sold Jack Daniel's is a black label, in which the text is a recovery of old brands that appear in the cooked earth jars that once served as packaging. On the other hand, a much rarer one, which has a green label, is slightly less alcoholic (42.8% versus 44.5% for the first). The distillery also produces another whiskey, with the name of Lem et Motlow sold mostly in Tennessee and Georgia.

Jack Daniel's advertising, has not been changed after decades, this has contributed in large part to its success in the United States, and later in the export. Using only black and white, in picturesque photos of Lynchburg, with its 360 inhabitants and the distillery workers, and making known all that is «the spirit» of Jack Daniel's: tradition, patience, quality. All people are authentic, genuine and do not pretend. On the other hand, society has given rise to a very strong club, the Tennessee Squire Association. With the exact number of affiliates, all fervent lovers of Jack Daniel's, the entity of each of them is jealously guarded in secret, but it is known that among them are actors, athletes and politicians.

These partners receive a small plot of land in the distillery and become citizens of honor of the city. Above all, they can go for a glass of Jack Daniel's in a private distillery room. A rare privilege in the town, like the whole county, is «dry», meaning that it is forbidden to buy and drink alcohol, including Jack Daniel's.

Jim Beam

Type: **bourbon.**
Origin: **Clermont (Kentucky).**
Owner: **American Brands.**
Date of birth: **1795.**

Although they are of German origin, the Beam could be Scottish since they constitute a very broad clan, in which many of their members worked in the whiskey industry. The brand has derived in numerous variants, not only in bourbon but also in rye. The most distant known ancestor is one M. Bohm. But nobody knows exactly when he Americanized his name, or when he went to Maryland to settle in Kentucky. The first known distiller in the family, Jacob Beam, worked from 1795 not far from Louisville, but it was not until 1800 that David Beam, one of his grandchildren, founded the Clermont distillery, near the source of Clear Springs.

Jim Beam, his son, gave his name to the best-selling bourbon brand in the United States and in the world. Its progression was constant, to the point of needing to acquire a second distillery, implanted a few kilometers away, not far from the town of Nelson. But society put on its labels as address... «Beam, Kentucky», simply.

It is not easy to produce the same whiskey in two different distilleries, but the members of the family guarantee its quality since they are the ones who supervise the production in each one of them. They currently represent the sixth generation of the Beam in producing this bourbon and

One of Jack Daniel's aging stores.

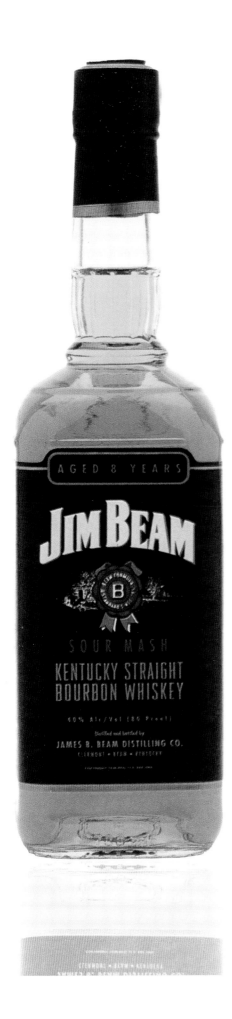

many other members of the family work in the company but also with the rival producers.

Anyway, the company no longer belongs to the Beam, it was bought in 1967 by the American Brands group, which owns not only other brands of whiskeys but also has interests in tobacco and other activities.

In addition, the distillery and the cellars of Clermont are located near a Baptist church and its cemetery, which ensures a great calm for the aging of bourbon; the numerous visitors go over the whole museum, which gathers a quite impressive collection of carafes created by the brand. There are many hundreds, from glass and plastic, to porcelain. Their forms are very varied, reproducing especially cars, trains, animals, politicians, etc. Each year new models are created and there is a collectors' club, formed by more than a thousand members. The range of whiskeys is very broad. The bourbons are the most numerous, but there is also a pure rye that has a yellow label.

The best-known and most exported Jim Beam is distinguished by a white label. It's a four-year-old bourbon, bottled with 40% alcohol. Very soft, it has as a distinctive sign, typical throughout the production of the group, a long and strong ending. Its harmony is given by the yeast used in the fermentation of cereals, which brings a lot of sweetness in relation to the *sour mash* process.

The Beam's Choice with green label, also called «No. 8 », experiences a prolonged aging of one year. As for the Beam with black label, it is bottled at 45% alcohol, after an aging of at least eight

years. The producer prefers to say that it has one hundred one month (almost eight and a half years), this makes it very chic and above all it can be confused with an alcohol content of 101° (around 50%). Its aromatic complexity is very developed.

These different qualities can also undergo important variations according to the markets where they are marketed.

Maker's Mark

Type: **bourbon.**
Origin: **Loretto (Kentucky).**
Owner: **Samuels.**
Date of birth: **1953.**

This bourbon puts the word «whisky», in his bottle, it is not a misspelling or a printing error. The Samuels family differs, in this point as in many others, from the rest of the rivals, and is the only Kentucky bourbon that restores the Scottish or Canadian title. Their Star Hill Farm distillery is the smallest in Kentucky and certainly in all the United States, its production does not exceed a few dozens of barrels per day. Its foundation goes back to 1805, but the current buildings date from the end of the last century. The antiquity of the installation, but also its rural charm (like its painted shutters), have earned it a recognition as a historic monument.

The Samuels have been distillers for four generations in Kentucky, as indicated by the «IV» that appears in Roman numerals on the label of their bourbon, but they have worked at Star Hill Farm only since 1953, when they bought the distillery. The history of the family has marked the United States many times. One of the Samuels was the grandfather of Jesse and Frank James, the famous gangsters of the last century. Another employed in the distillery Abraham Lincoln's father. Bill Samuels, who bought the distillery in 1953, went out of his way to take advantage of the artisanal character of Maker's Mark. The small size of the company allowed him to perfectly control the water quality as well as the cereals that are used: mainly corn, with a little rye or wheat. Its cooking is done slowly, a luxury that large producers cannot afford. After aging, which lasts an average of six years, the barrels are regularly changed at different levels, so that the result is homogeneous in each one of them.

The packaging wants to reflect a traditional character, since the cap of each bottle is sealed, a job that can only be done manually.

The Knob Creek whiskey is distilled in Clermont, Kentucky and this one has matured for nine years in barrels more intensely burned by coal, category 4 «Alligator». In this way, Whiskey can extract the richest vanilla and most natural sugars from timber.

This bourbon very soft and with a great finesse has been baptized as the Rolls-Royce of whiskies and above all... of whiskeys. The most current version, sealed in red, has 45% alcohol. There is another, with 50.5% that looks wax and labels in gold.

Although the distillery has always been run by the Samuels family, the Hiram Walker group currently owns a part, which facilitates Maker's Mark exports.

Old Crow

Type: **bourbon.**
Origin: **Frankfort (Kentucky).**
Owner: **National Distillers.**
Date of birth: **1835.**

Despite the bird that adorns the label (especially the one destined for export), the brand has nothing to do with the crow, but with its founder, the Scottish James Crow, who settled in Kentucky in the first half of the nineteenth century. The buildings have retained a bit of the British aspect.

The brand claims to be the inventor of the *sour mash* process, which is possible given its age, but it cannot be proven with historical documents. The Old Crow in any case does not need such legitimation: this very classic bourbon is popular in the United States and begins to be exported. Michael Jackson qualifies him as the bourbon «for every day», this statement is not to disqualify it, but to make understand how nice it is. The most common is that bottled at 40% alcohol, but there is a 50% version.

Old Grand Dad

Type: **bourbon.**
Origin: **Frankfort (Kentucky).**
Owner: **National Distillers.**
Date of birth: **1882.**

Although the brand dates back to 1882, the current distillery dates back to 1901, and is the most industrial distillery in the city of Frankfort. A premium corn, a yeast before prohibition and an incredible dexterity in aging form a bourbon of quality, fruity and strong at the same time. It is normally bottled at 43%, but there is a stronger quality at 50.5%, with an aging of eight to ten years.

Overholt

Type: **rye whiskey.**
Origin: **Frankfort (Kentucky).**
Owner: **National Distillers.**
Date of birth: **1810.**

Made primarily from rye, rye whiskey has long been an important part of US production. But, since the Second World War, consumers left it a little aside; this triggered a considerable drop in sales and, consequently, the closure of numerous distilleries.

Pennsylvania and Maryland were the main producing states of rye; currently, the remaining distilleries brewed their whiskeys in the style of bourbon. The last remaining rye brands come from Kentucky.

This is the case of Overholt. The family has German origin and arrived in Pennsylvania at the beginning of the 18th century. They were weavers by profession, but they made their own whiskey for personal consumption. One of the sons, Abraham, created a distillery in 1810 in Westmoreland county. The brand remained in the hands of the family until the 1930s. Its rye is highly valued as it contains up to 59% rye, although the law only requires 51%.

The prohibition in the city along with the discredit before the Americans triggered the closing of the society. But such a beautiful brand could not disappear forever and was purchased by National Distillers. Distillation and aging take place in Frankfort, Kentucky.

With Jim Beam yellow label (plus some small labels), Overholt is the last great rye brand that still exists, and the whiskey lovers knows it for its particular taste. Carrying the prefix of old, it is bottled at 43% alcohol, but also at 46.5%, in an old version that can still be found to some collectors.

Schenley OFC

Type: **Canadian blend.**
Origin: **Valleyfield (Québec).**
Owner: **Schenley.**
Date of birth: **1948.**

The distillery is located on the shore of Saint-Laurent, just opposite the United States, which clearly indicates the origins of this Canadian group. Indeed in its beginnings it was a subsidiary of the American group with the same name, installed in Louisville (Kentucky), which on the other hand reduced its activity in the sector of the spirits.

Created in 1948, the Canadian group took its financial independence in 1981, before being bought by Canadian United Distillers in 1990. The distillery of Valleyfield, the only one of the group, is today the second in the country for its production, with 34,000 tons of cereals treated every year and thirteen aging stores. Produced in a classic Canadian style and main brand of the group, the Schenley OFC (that is «Original Fine Canadian») is an eight-year blend, commercialized since 1955 and which has won numerous medals and awards. It is not the only reference of the group, on the other hand it is also surprising that different whiskeys are produced in the same distillery. The other particularity of Schenley, a fairly recent group, is to market whiskeys much older than their rivals.

There is a whole series of popular whiskeys, first prizes, such as the Golden Wedding, 909, Three Lancers, Bon Vivant, etc. The Gibson's Finest, with an aging of twelve years, is an important brand, appreciated for its softness. Schenley Award is a ten years, and exists under the brand Park & Tilford a blend of about eighteen years. For his twenty-fifth anniversary in 1973, Schleny produced a limited series of carafes containing a blend made from the oldest whiskeys it had in stock, between seventeen and twenty years. Currently, it is a very sought product by collectors.

Seagram's V.O.

Type: **Canadian blend.**
Origin: **Waterloo (Ontario).**
Owner: **Seagram.**
Date of birth: **1857.**

Creating a milling mill after a small distillery near Toronto, the Seagram family (of British origin) could not imagine that a century later it would give its name to the first worldwide distillation and distribution group of spirits. The truth is that the success lies entirely in one man, Samuel Bronfman. The Seagram family was appreciated for its rye whiskey, of which it becomes the first producer. In 1920, the family company was bought by the Scottish group DCL, which sought to establish itself in North America. For this, it is associated with Bronfman. Of Russian origin, at the beginning they were dealing with liquors in general, then they launch into the world of whiskey creating a distillery in La Salle, near Montreal.

But the ban changed the minds of the Scottish leaders of DCL, who preferred to withdraw from the American market, since they did not want to take the path of illegality. Samuel Bronfman did not think the same, used hidden means (Newfoundland or Havana) to supply smugglers, in parallel, from 1928, began to age whiskey in large quantities, because he was sure that the dry regime would not last forever. In 1933, he demonstrated he was right, and he took the lead all over the world: he could flood the American market, where there were no stocks, while the Scots were not ready. Bronfman won an incredible fortune that he was constantly reinvesting. He bought distilleries in the United States, then in Scotland, also producing other spirits such as rum, gin, vodka, etc.

In Canada, the group became the leading producer of whiskeys, with six distilleries and a large number of brands. The most important is the Seagram's V.O., a six-year blend made with more than a hundred different whiskies. Samuel Bronfman was not only a brilliant businessman, he was also

passionate about whiskey and was particularly interested in blending techniques. This was the basis of the most important development for him to produce perfect products at both aromatic and flavor levels

In Canada, the other main references of the group are the Lord Calvert; the Harwood, lighter; James Foxe; the Adam's, of which there are versions of twelve and eight years.

On the other hand, it owns Hudson's Bay Distillers and makes the whiskeys marketed by Jack Baker. Many of these brands are exported to the United States, especially in bulk. It is on the other hand in the United States, in New York, where is the most beautiful symbol of the Seagram empire: a spectacular building made by Mies van der Rohe in the 50s.

Wild Turkey

Type: **bourbon.**
Origin: **Lawrenceburg (Kentucky).**
Owner: **Austin Nichols
(Grand Metropolitan)**
Date of birth: **1855.**

Wild Turkey has obtained the Gold Award in 1992.

The best-selling quality in the United States is 50.5% alcohol, with an aging of eight years, but, in export, 43.4% alcohol is marketed. There is also in the same brand a rye, and also a liquor in which Wild Turkey is added with honey and lemon. With great strength, the Wild Turkey is a category bourbon and very aromatic.

The Wild Turkey distillery in Lawrenceburg.

As in Scotland with The Famous Grouse, the United States has a brand that bears the name of a bird that appears as a national emblem, the wild turkey. It almost became the symbol of the recent United States, especially proposed by Benjamin Franklin, but finally the eagle was chosen... Although, the turkey is always the main course of the Thanksgiving Day menu, this national and family holiday that takes place the fourth Thursday of November. It remembers the arrival of the first settlers of the *Mayflower* in the year 1620, and the thanksgiving meal, one year after their arrival.

Originally from North America, the wild turkey is a bird a little more impressive than its domestic variant, weighs about ten kilos and can measure up to 1.20 m in height. Flying, it reaches 90 km/h. His discovery caused a sensation, and the first specimens taken to Europe were very successful, especially when they were served at the table of the king of France Charles IX calling them «Indian roosters», which gave rise to his current denomination. Because of its strength and ability, it is a very appreciated piece by American hunters. The fact of celebrating Thanksgiving and the demand for turkeys meant that the species was about to disappear in the course of the 19th century. Today it is the object of effective protection.

The origins of the bourbon of the same name are less clear. Some know well the story of the brothers James and John Ripy, two Irish who settled in Lawrenceburg, Kentucky, in 1851. At first, they opened a grocery store, then created a distillery in 1855, when there were already several in the city. It is true that the place was recognized for many years for the quality and abundance of its water. The distillery was moved twice, in 1873 and then in 1905, in order to prevent flooding of the Kentucky River. Finally, it was settled on the top of a hill called Wild Turkey. Anyway, according to Michael Jackson, the brand is not originally from Lawrenceburg, and his name owes nothing to the Ripy brothers. It was launched by the Austin Nichols society. According to an anecdote, it would be a wild turkey hunter who asked a distiller of society to create a whiskey with this name to surprise his friends. In 1971 Austin Nichols became the owner of the Lawrenceburg distillery. Once owned by the French company Pernod (which is always its distributor in France), Austin Nichols belonged to Heublein, before being bought by Grand Metropolitan.

In any case, in our days, Wild Turkey is a true bourbon, produced within the rules of Lawrenceburg art. It is also one of the best-selling premiums in the United States, and exports reached 300,000 boxes in 1993.

Benchmark

This very soft and pleasantly scented bourbon is made by Seagram in his distillery in Lawrenceburg, Kentucky. The proportion of corn used is 60%, and aging is at least six years.

Canadian's Tippers

With five years of age, this brand of Canadian whiskey is directed towards the French market on behalf of the distributor William Peters, of Bordeaux.

Eagle Rare

Prepared by Seagram, this bourbon has taken its name from the American national emblem. It is made in the same distillery as the Benchmark.

Early Times

Distilled in Louisville, it is one of the lightest and clearest bourbons that ex-

ist, it belongs to the Brown Forman society. Arriving in the city, you can see a giant bottle of Early Times that dominates the distillery. But don't be enthusiastic, since the replica only contains water, which serves as a fire reserve.

Evan Williams

Carrying the name of one of the oldest distillers in Kentucky, this bourbon is made

in Bardstown, Kentucky, by the Heaven Hill distillery. It dates back to 1783, but its activities were really resumed after the ban in 1935. Very aromatic and of great strength, this bourbon is filtered in charcoal after an aging of four years for 40% alcohol, and from ten years to 50%. There is also a range of bourbons that bear the Heaven Hill brand.

Ezra Brooks

This brand of bourbon has gone through many vicissitudes. It was born in the distillery of the Medley family, founded in Lebanon, Kentucky, at the beginning of the last century. It then emigrated to Daviess County, before being reborn in Owensboro after the ban. The Medley launched the brand in the mid-50s, copying a little Jack Daniel's, then out of stock. The latter brand sued them in response. Ezra Brooks changed hands many times, before becoming the property of David Sherman, of Saint Louis, Missouri. They propose a version of 45% alcohol, but there is a 50.5% and seven years old, called Old Ezra, which has much more character.

Forester

According to its owner, the Brown Forman company, this bourbon made in Louisville was one of the first to be bottled, because its creator, George Brown, could not stand that his whiskey was delivered in barrels as it was styled and that was manipulated, even distorted, by the bartenders. It was developed from 1870 with the Old Forester brand, but the current managers estimate that the «old» appeal is not appropriate and they removed it from the label, especially for export. On the other hand, the bottle always carries the reproduction of the guarantee handwritten by George Brown certifying the quality of his bourbon. Currently his great-grandchildren run the company, which also owns Jack Daniel's and Southern Comfort.

George Dickel

Of German origin, George Dickel is installed as a merchant of spirits in Nashville (Tennessee) from 1863 and seven years later was already a distiller. He put into practice an original formula of cold filtration on charcoal from a particular species of maple syrup. In 1879, he built a new distillery in Tullahoma, called «Waterfall». Dickel died in 1894, and his whiskey was a great success until the ban. This began in 1910 in Tennessee, forcing the company to totally close and sell its stocks for medicinal use. The Waterfall distillery was not reopened until 1958 by the Schenley group, after the increasing success of Jack Daniel's, which used the same process as George Dickel's.

The George Dickel whiskey (the name Waterfall was dismissed), particularly mild, exists mainly in a 43.4° version. The company currently belongs to United Distillers.

James E. Pepper

It is an excellent bourbon manufactured by the Bernheim distillery in Louisville, Kentucky. Unfortunately, nowadays it is difficult to find since it was produced in small quantities.

John Lee

This Kentucky bourbon of eight years is distributed mainly in France by the company Bardinet, associated shortly before La Martiniquaise, specialist in sales of large distribution.

Old Fitzgerald

Founded in the beginning in Frankfort, the distillery was installed in Louisville since 1870. Its range (even up to twelve years old) has great strength and beautiful elegance.

Old Peel

It has the name similar to other spirits (the scotch William Peel for example), this bourbon of eight years is made in the United States by the French William Pitters, who deals with the large distribution.

Old Taylor

Owned by National Distillers, this Frankfort bourbon is named after its founder, Colonel Taylor. It is made in a surprising distillery that looks like a medieval castle with towers and fortifications, which could become a bourbon museum. Quite light in structure, Old Taylor bourbon is of great aromatic finesse.

Old Virginia

Distilled and aged in the United States, this eight-year bourbon reserved for the French market is distributed mainly in large distribution by the company La Martiniquaise.

Rebel Yell

William Weller and his brothers were not only Louisville distillers, but also ardent southerners. They enlisted in the ranks of the Confederate army during the Civil War, officially becoming rebels. They resumed their activities after the failure. Their bourbon has the distinction of not using rye, but it has a bit of wheat in its composition. Rebel Yell was from the beginning a little extended brand, only for family and good friends. After the ban, the successors of the Weller brothers were associated with the Stitzel distillery. The distribution of Rebel Yell developed little by little, although for a long time it was limited to the southern states that formed the Confederation. It was in the 80s when it spread throughout the country, since the natives of the south were changing state and pretend Rebel Yell where they passed. Sweet and very clear,

Rebel Yell ages for at least seven years in oak barrels. It currently belongs to United Distillers.

Royal Reserve

This Canadian whiskey, presented as a rye whiskey, is the best-selling brand of the Corby distillery, one of the oldest in the country, located in Belleville, near Toronto. Although in 1907 it was destroyed by a fire, it was later rebuilt preserving the old style and currently still maintains its charm. Specializing in the production of light whiskeys, today belongs to the Hiram Walker group.

Ten High

Distilled in Bardstown, in Kentucky, this bourbon of great quality knew its maximum success in the American military bases installed in Europe after the Second World War. Its export had a resurgence since the beginning of the 90s.

Van Winkle

This great family of bourbon distillers of Louisville, among which the famous " "papa Van Winkle", who worked for the Stitzel-Weller, is honored by an excellent bourbon, at 53.5°. This bourbon is hard to find, but it is nevertheless a true marvel.

Virginia Gentleman

There are almost no Virginia whiskeys left, but this keeps the tradition. The Smith Bowman Distillery was founded in Fredericksburg after the ban, in 1935, and is currently managed by General Lee's great-grandson. Its whiskey has a beautiful elegance with great strength in its flavor.

Yellowstone

On its label appears the famous geyser of Yellowstone National Park, the best known in the United States, but this bourbon is nothing more than a tourist curiosity. It was created in 1886 by an old family of distillers, the Dant, installed in Kentucky since 1836. Since then, the brand has changed hands many times, before becoming in 1993 owned by David Sherman, of Saint Luis, Missouri

The 40°, 43° and 45°, are very nice bourbons, not very aggressive and especially charming.

SOUTHERN COMFORT

Americans have no great traditions in whiskey liquors, and the Southern Comfort is a notable exception that reflects a true culture. Made from bourbon, peaches, oranges and aromatic herbs, this liquor is consumed with ice, giving the glass a southern air of Deep South, the deep south of yesteryear. Its existence recalls the links between Kentucky and the southern states: bourbon came from Ohio and ships sailing on the Mississippi were dismantled upon their arrival in Louisiana. The result of the sale was to buy horses that took the Kentucky road. Here, the green meadows transformed them into superb racehorses. The Southern Comfort, made in Saint Luis, Missouri, is currently part of the Brown Forman group.

THE REFINEMENTS OF THE EMPIRE

Because of their alphabet and their religion coming from China, cameras and tape recorders from Europe and computers from the United States, the Japanese are always represented as simple imitators, incapable of the least creativity. In the matter of drinks, the same thing happens. If sake, a fermented rice drink, is a national reference, beer and whiskey have been copied of the West to be made in situ.

But the Japanese also have the secret of perfectionism. Their copies always exceed the original, becoming true references in the field. It happens the same with their whiskeys.

It is from Scotland that the Japanese took their skills and since then they were totally faithful to this model: double distillation in pot still, use of peat, blending with some grain whiskeys and aging in sherry or bourbon casks.

The Japanese specificity of whiskey is not obvious, and for a long time it has been easy to denigrate Japanese production, as has often been done in Europe... it has taken time to taste the many whiskeys produced there. Following Michael Jackson *(The World Guide to Whisky)*, specialists now agree to recognize that Japanese whiskeys have a good quality, and especially a true style, some close to scotch.

JAPAN

It is the merit of the Japanese distillers that they developed the quality of their whiskeys when they had a captive market and that they had no intention of competing in the export with the Scots or the Canadians. Now, after having marketed their blends of good quality, they begin the adventure of «single malt», with very long aging. Their only weakness is undoubtedly the small number of their distilleries (less than ten): although they are capable of producing different types of whiskeys, they are far from the great diversity of Highlands, including the composition of the blends. Taking up the words of Michael Jackson, the Scottish blenders have the symphonic orchestra of Beethoven, and their Japanese colleagues only have the string quartet of Vivaldi.

The passion of Japanese distillers for Scotland has increased when they have been able to become owners of Highlands distilleries. Nikka bought Ben Nevis in 1989, and Suntory owns interests in Morrison-Bowmore. A very qualitative choice, as seen... In Japan, the time of the whiskey is especially at the exit of the offices, in the multiple bars that there are around the great stations and places of leisure. If the glass of scotch or bourbon is generally small in size, barely capable of containing the usual dose added to a little fresh water, the Japanese is served in a large glass and diluted in plenty of water and ice, up to four or five times 3 centiliters of the base dose. A practice that forces the distillers to elaborate whiskeys of certain aromatic power... Its consumption is reserved to men and constitutes above all an essential social rite. Drinking a whiskey in a bar near work is almost as important as having worked hard all day. Eventually, the party of the night will continue with a dinner, then with new libations during a karaoke contest. It is not strange that the whiskey, always watered down, accompanies the meals. There are many culinary affinities between the sushi and other fish dishes and whiskey that would not deny a real Scotsman. It is not surprising to see how Japan figures in the first places in the production and consumption of whiskey.

Masataka Taketsuru, the true father of Japanese whiskey (at first with Suntory, later in his society Nikka), in the company of his Scottish wife, Rita.

They are different because of a clean taste, a class of refined elegance with perfectly assimilated aromas. They do not have the power of the Islay whiskeys nor the vigor of some Speyside products. The use of peat, especially, is moderate, without ever being totally absent. The creation of the first Japanese distillery by Suntory, in 1923 in Yamazaki, is in itself a symbol. Since it is set in a mountainous region, very rich in good quality fountains, it could perfectly remind a landscape of Highlands.

Currently, to meet demand, Japanese distillers are obliged to import most of their raw materials (barley and peat especially), the water quality of the archipelago plays an essential role in the production of their whiskeys, even if they did not have the peaty aromas that constitute the specific style of scotch.

On this basis, the Japanese have built a powerful whiskey industry, although it is not very expanded. Suntory and its twenty different brands represent around 70% of the national production, a true giant on a world scale.

It is mainly consumed in the archipelago, whose population amounts to about 125 million inhabitants. And, until these last years, they had almost no will to make the Japanese production known to the rest of the world. This attitude, radically different from that of the other world producers, arises in parallel with the strong limitations imposed on the importation of foreign whiskeys by a very dissuasive rate system.

Nikka

Is the passion of Japanese distillers for Scotland the fruit of a love story? The story of Nikka and its founder, Masataka Taketsuru, seems to prove it. Son of a sake makers saga that dates back to the seventeenth century was passionate about Scotch whiskey, but also throughout Scotland, to the point of marrying a young Scottish, Jessie Roberta Cowan, who would follow him to Japan where he was the inspirer of the main producers of whiskey.

Born in 1894, Taketsuru has learned from his family the art of making sake, his father said that "the artist's soul is reflected in the sake he makes". Passionate about studies, he became interested in all forms of fermentation and distillation. In 1918,

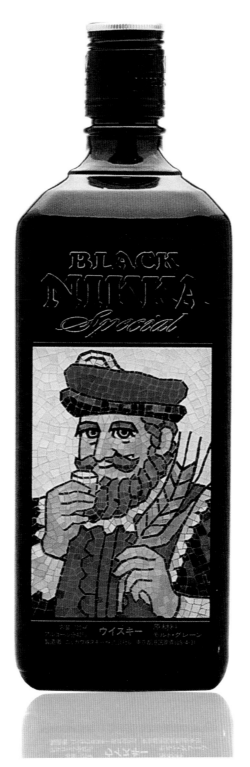

Rita Taketsuru, born in Scotland, lived more than forty years in Japan.

taking advantage of a treaty between Great Britain and Japan, he went to the University of Glasgow to complete his training and became the first Japanese to study whiskey in Scotland. He also worked at a distillery, which could be Glen Grant in Rothes, or maybe The Glenlivet. But nowadays, nobody has proof of this in their archives... There is also a photo of Taketsuru in front of the distillery portal of White Horse. The studies do not prevent the feelings of Taketsuru from surfacing; at twenty-six, he meets Jessie Roberta Cowan, nicknamed Rita, who was twenty-four years old and lived with her family outside of Glasgow. Despite her shyness, the Scotswoman could not resist the charms of the stranger who came from the other part of the world. A few months later, they marry, despite the implacable opposition from their families, and must settle for a simple statement in a Glasgow municipal office.

In November 1920, the Taketsuru couple returned to Japan. They settle at the beginning in Osaka, but the society that had sent the young Japanese to study the art of whiskey has changed his mind, and at the end separated from him. For a while, it is Rita who keeps the couple, giving English lessons. Then, Taketsuru is hired by Shinjiro Torii, the founder of the Suntory group, who is looking for a true whiskey professional. His task will be to build the first distillery of the group, in Yamazaki.

Taketsuru wants to fly with his own wings and, in July 1934, he creates his own distillation company, Dai-Nippon Kaju K.K. (called today Nikka) which is established in Yoichi, on the northern island of Hokkaido. The region is mountainous and the climate rigorous, but everything reminds of Scotland, even several peat bogs. The first still arrives in 1935 (Nikka must wait for many years before having the means to own a second) and Rita meets her husband soon after. The first whiskey mix was made by Ta-

ketsuru in 1939, and the commercialization took place a year later, some twenty years after his return to Japan.

They are going through a war, and times are hard, especially for Rita. Despite her Japanese citizenship, she must endure the police inconvenience because she is European. But she will continue her whole life faithful to her husband and to Japan, never returning to Scotland, on the pretext that she cannot stand the plane. The couple does not have children, but adopt nephews

of Taketsuru, who continue in this way the family dynasty. Rita only sees one of her sisters once, in 1959, before dying in 1961. She is buried on the top of a hill next to Yoichi's distillery, where her husband will join her eighteen years later.

True father of the Japanese whiskey, Taketsuru has contributed without any doubt to print the Scottish style that never left. His company is currently the second in production in Japan. It has two distilleries, Yoichi and Miyagikyo, also located in the north of

The Yoichi distillery, the oldest of the Nikka group.

the archipelago, in a region reminiscent of the Lowlands. Its pagoda-shaped chimneys have nothing Oriental, but remember Scotland. It is also a producer of liqueurs and alcohol based on apples, and a distributor of imported wines and spirits. Owner of the Scottish distillery Ben Nevis (founded by the legendary Long John McDonald), the group also owns the Dompierre distillery in Cognac.

Nikka faithfully follows the teachings received by Masataka Taketsuru in Scotland: distillation of malted barley in traditional stills, aging in oak casks, blending. The range, quite wide, includes especially a blend, with the name «The Blend», which comprises at least 50% of malt whiskey; the Super Nikka, one of the most sold, which is said to have been created by Taketsuru as «a requiem in memory of his wife after her death»; a «pure malt», called «All Malt»; a «single malt» of twelve years; the Black Nikka, in a curious black bottle, one of the first light blends of Japan. The star is Tsuru, a superb blend using old malts, of great softness and superior finish. It is packed in a white porcelain carafe of a perfect design, adorned with raised cranes. Diminutive of the founder of Nikka, the word *tsuru*, in Japanese, actually designates the crane. There are many other presentations, in very different packaging, since the Japanese love this variety in styles and packaging.

Suntory

In 1899, at the age of twenty-one, Shinjiro Torii set up a wine business in Osaka, imported at the beginning from Spain. Twenty years ago, Emperor Mutsuhito come to power, and with it began the Meiji era. After centuries of complete isolation and strict maintenance of their traditions, the country of the Rising Sun opened to the outside world. Torii was one of the golden boys of the time, he was passionate about the western world and its products.

In the name of his society, Suntory, you can read the association of his own name, in English «tory», with the English word *sun*, the emblem of Japan. In 1907, he marketed his first own brand, a sweet red wine, near the port, called Akadama, and gets down to work to create other spirits in the western style, such as liqueurs or brandies.

In 1923, the group decided to take an interest in whiskey and built the first distillery in Japan, in Yamazaki, a valley located in the mountains between Osaka and Kyoto. He invited the expert of Masataka Taketsuru, the first Japanese to have studied whiskey in Scotland. At the moment, its name does not appear in the official history of the group, since Taketsuru left it some years later to found Nikka, its main rival. One must take into account Torii's blender talent and his qualities as a taster, very accurate characteristics.

The first whiskey, called Suntory Shirofuda (which corresponds to the current Suntory White), was marketed from 1929. It would be followed by numerous products of an increasing level of quality.

Yamazaki's situation was not only chosen because of its resemblance to the Highlands landscape. The climate, cold and humid, was ideal for the aging of whiskey in casks.

Since, from its origins, Suntory tried to approach the Scottish model as much as possible. Currently, two different distillation lines allow the production of different whiskeys.

The real launch of Japanese whiskey did not take place until after the Second World War, once prosperity returned. Meanwhile, the Suntory group was busy with beer, quickly becoming the country's fourth brewer.

In 1973, a second malt distillery was opened in Hakushu, in the middle of the mountain, in the center of Japan. With twenty-four *pot stills,* it is the most important in the world. This allows them to elaborate a more varied whiskeys, differing slightly by their shape from those of Yamazaki. It has its own aging store. The large pine forests that surround it are also a sanctuary

SUNTORY WHISK

THE ART OF JAPANESE WHISKY

SINCE 1923

THE JAPANESE CRAFT GIN

ROKU GIN
SELECT EDITION 6
700ml.

SUNTORY
UMESHU

Plum liqueur
matured in
the toasted cask in
YAMAZAKI

山崎蒸溜所貯蔵
焙煎樽熟成梅酒

リキュール 750ml

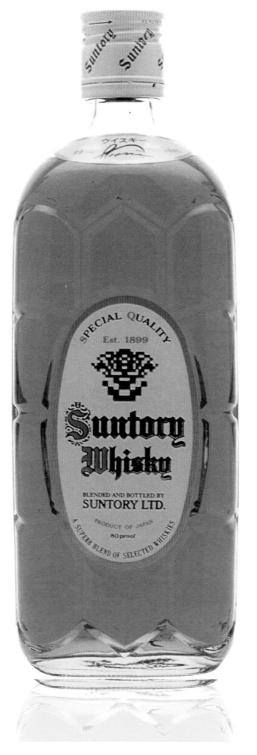

for birds. The place also houses a museum of whiskey and distillation in general, with pieces dating back to the fifteenth century. The abundance and crystalline purity of the Hakushu waters help to create a third malt distillery, opened in 1981. Suntory also has a grain distillery, in Chita, and its own malt (also used for the production of beers).

On the other hand, Suntory has not ceased to diversify: creation of vineyards, development in liquors (with its original Midori melon liquor, a true innovation in the sector) and soft drinks, but also in food products (frozen), medicines, etc. The company also has numerous chains of restaurants and stores, sports and leisure clubs, an editorial, etc. The total number of its sales exceeds 7 billion dollars in 1994, whiskey and wines and spirits (except beer) represent a little more than half.

The group is considerably developed abroad, becoming in this way one of the greats of the spirits business, such as Seagram or United Distillers. Suntory partnered with Allied Domecq and owns vineyards in California and in Bordelais (Lagrange and Beychevelle especially), breweries in China and in many countries in the Far East, a cognac distillery, business partnerships scattered on all sides, especially in United States, etc.

And yet it has remained a family majority; Shinchiro Torii, the founder's son, is the current president.

The Suntory Old, a slightly peaty blend, is the whiskey currently sold by the group. It comes from Yamazaki. The range of blends is one of the most varied, including SR (Suntory Royal), Reserve, Imperial, Excellence, Ibiki, Kakubin, etc. They are subtle and elegant variations of the same style, marked by their softness, fineness of flavor and aromatic qualities affirmed without being dominant.

In the 1980s, Suntory also marketed its first twelve-year «single malt» produced in Yamazaki. Later appeared other lighter whiskeys, made for younger consumers. Dominating the Japanese whiskey market, in which it represents around 70% of the national production, Suntory is also the Japanese group most introduced in the export of its brands, although it represents less than 5% of its total sales. Since, like all Japanese distillers, Suntory does not export almost its whiskeys, with difference from other world producers. Shyness, reserve or indifference? It is not known, but, with its commercial power and the quality of its whiskeys, if the group decided to make a decision, the others would have some concerns to face…

The superb stills of the Yamazaki distillery (Suntory).

AND ALSO...

Kirin-Seagram

The first Japanese brewer, Kirin, joined in the 70s the first world distiller, the Anglo-Canadian Seagram, to make some Japanese whiskeys using mostly Scottish methods: who said that the whiskey was a small world folded on itself? Kirin-Seagram evidently proves quite the opposite. Representing 4% of the Japanese market, it owns a distillery in the vicinity of Mount Fuji, where it produces both malts and a grain whiskey. It only markets its blends, aged in bourbon barrels, which are the driest and most peaty in Japan, with leading brands such as Crescent, Emblem, Robert Brown and News. Kirin-Seagram

also imports some Scottish malts to perfect their blends.

Sunraku Ocean

Despite its name, this small distillery is not located on the edge of the sea, but in the middle of the mountain in central Japan, in Karuizawa. It is also a leisure center appreciated by the most select of Japanese society for decades. Specializing in the wine business and the making of sake, the family that controls it was launched into the world of whiskey from the 30s, and especially since the Second World War. It also has a grain distillery, and many diversified activities in the agri-food industry. True to the Japanese style, its range of whiskeys is wide, with the «single malt» Karuizawa (without precise age) and the blends Asama (the richest), Sta-

tus, Ocean, or even the Route, the lighter, destined to the younger generations.

IN THE WHOLE WORLD

If scotch, bourbon, Canadian and Japanese whiskeys dominate the world for their respective qualities as for their volume, they are not the only ones, in terms of production at least. After all, the cereals that allow distilled spirits, of more or less quality, make their way around the world, and aging in wooden barrels is a matter of time... and especially money. It is not surprising that whiskeys are produced both in Germany and in India, in Australia or in South America, in Israel or in the Czech Republic. The same as in France, where the launch of the production of a Breton whiskey is regularly announced, which remains until now without continuity...

In any case, they lack the secular patience and skill that allow to select the ingredients perfectly, to control the market of the distillation and to constitute sufficient stocks.

These whiskeys on the other hand are more or less «enriched» with others sold in bulk from Scotland or Canada, as they do not have a satisfactory level of flavor by themselves. And their market is limited to their regional, even national, borders. Sometimes quite rude, they are above all of great banality and obviously do not suffer comparison with the world elite.

In India, for example, whiskey is, since the English colonization, the alcoholic beverage of reference, even the only one consumed, particularly in large parties and important events.

For many years, the importation of foreign whiskeys (such as Scots) has been banned, in order to limit currency evasion. This attitude has generated the development of a local production of a quality that is sometimes barely acceptable. Since recently, the market has change, but this opportunity does not like the world's leaders. Like Johnnie Walker, who imagines his fame there, the brands fear that some bottles they sell are mostly reused to present their local, banal or even dangerous mixtures, thus ruining their image.

GUIDE

Cereals, water, a distillation system, barrels: the manufacture of whiskey, like brandy, is quite simple in principle as its ingredients and the necessary equipment. But it is a set of conditions, sometimes insignificant in appearance, that can differentiate a banal alcohol and a great whiskey. Every technical detail counts, but also, and above all, the touch of the master distiller in the crucial stage of the still.

The making of a whiskey cannot be improvised. First of all, you should take your time, not only to learn the trade and improve your skills permanently, but also because the slow transformation that starts from cereal grains to get a tasty amber liquid takes several years.

A *washback*, fermentation tank made of pine wood, from the Wild Turkey distillery.

THE CEREALS

Barley is the most interesting cereal to make whiskey: it is rich in starch capable of transforming into fermentable sugars. Moreover, the envelope that covers the grain constitutes a natural filter once the mixture has finished. In short, this cereal grows better in the more northern areas where others fail to develop.

Also the barley is always present, in any type of whiskey manufactured. Even to distill the grain whiskey, it is necessary to add a little malted barley to facilitate the operations. It is sometimes used raw, but it is the malting that allows the maximum potential of the barley to be used. This operation is able to release enzymes that allow the transformation of starch into usable sugars. Once harvested, the barley begins to germinate under the influence of heat and a little moisture.

On the other hand, the germination operation takes place in large closed rooms where the grains are distributed in layers. It is necessary to move them in order to ensure that the germination is homogeneous. Most distilleries carry out these operations themselves, but currently the malting is done more often in large automated units.

Once the germination has finished, which may take one or two weeks, the barley is dried, then roasted to obtain the malt. It is in this state where the peat intervenes, at least in Scotland. The drying is in fact done, sometimes completely, sometimes in part, on two peat coal fires, in ovens on which go pagoda chimneys, the *kilns*. They do not have any oriental origin, but simply this form ensures the best leak of fumes. Although they do not do any service since the distilleries do not perform the malting, many in Scotland have been conserved, because they clearly indicate the existence of a distillery.

The king grain of the distillation of whiskey, barley is also the most expensive, therefore the malting increases even more the cost of production. Therefore, other cereals, such as wheat, corn, rye, even oats, have also been used. But they give less strong and less aromatic brandy compared to malted barley.

MIX

Crushed, that is to say, coarsely ground, the cereals undergo a mixture exactly the same as for brewing. They are added to hot water, at various intervals, in large tanks equipped with agitator blades. The operation is repeated many times, in order to extract the maximum sugars from the cereals. After the filtration, one obtains on the one hand the wort, a very dense sweetened juice, and on the other hand some solid particles, the residues of the barley. Its richness in proteins and cellulose make it a very appreciated food for cattle breeders. The percentage of alcohol obtained for the distillation will depend on the density of sugars in the wort, and that is why it is carefully measured, even by the tax men, to avoid fraud.

THE FERMENTATION

Once cold, the wort must ferment, with yeasts identical to those used in the brewery. With the action of the yeasts, the sugars are converted into alcohol and carbon dioxide. The operation, which lasts two and a half days, is carried out in large open vats, the *washbacks,* once made of pine wood (in Oregon it was the most appreciated of the distillers) and could contain 10,000 to 20,000 liters, and sometimes plus. At the end of the fermentation, which must be the object of great vigilance, especially as regards temperature, the liquid obtained will be between 8 and 10°. It is often called «beer» in distilleries.

DISTILLATION

The goal of the distillation is to increase the alcohol content of the fermented liquid by eliminating most of the water it contains, with the action of heat. In any case, this distillation (also called rectification) cannot be total, since the alcohol obtained would have neither aromas nor flavor. It is made, as for the other spirits, according to two different processes (but can be combined, as in Ireland) using specific stills.

Distillation in a still. It is the oldest known process, and is often used in Scotland to make malt whiskey.

It is developed in two times (as for cognac), in copper stills, the *pot stills,* heated either directly (with coal or gas), or by the mediation of coils where the boiling water vapor circulates. The first still is usually a little larger than the second.

With the heat, the fermented juice starts to boil. Alcohol, lighter than water, is the first to reach the top of the still and pass through the conduit to reach the condenser, a coil cooled in water. The obtained liquids, called *low* wine, have a percentage of alcohol around 25 to 30% and still contain many impurities.

Then it is taken to the second still, where the same heating operation is carried out. Here comes into play the skill of the distiller. At the beginning, the liquid obtained after condensation is still loaded with undesirable elements to obtain a good brandy (esters, aldehydes, volatile acids, etc.). These «distillation heads», must be eliminated, which are returned to the still. At one point, they were replaced by the «heart of distillation», the good quality liquor that is sought. Its quality is controlled especially by adding a little distilled water (which causes a confusing action also of the heads of the distillation) and measuring its density in alcohol.

At the end of the process appear the «distillation tails», which are equally harmful to obtain a good whiskey, and which are distributed in the still. All the art of the distiller is to know in what moments the heads and tails of distillation must be eliminated, in order to preserve the heart of the desired distillation. The character of this heart varies from one distillery to another, giving alcohols more or less laden with secondary products that make a difference in aroma and strength. For reasons that have never been fully elucidated, the size and shape of the stills play a large role in the aromatic characteristics of the spirits. The capacity, height and shape of the duct as the length of the coil also influence. Of course, when changing a used still (at twenty or thirty years in general), it is carefully copied in order to maintain the style of the whiskey. It is necessary to use six hours to distill from 6,000 to 7,000 liters of liqueur, between 60 and 70° according to the distilleries.

Suntory aging cellar in Japan.

THE DIFFERENT SYSTEMS OF MEASURING THE ALCOHOL DEGREE

From Gay-Lussac, the measurement of the degree of alcohol represents the volume, in percentage, of alcohol contained in a liquid, measured at 20°C. That is to say, a liter of alcohol with 40° (or also 40?») contains 40 centiliters of pure alcohol. For a long time, the British have used another, more complex system. It is no longer officially in force with European unification, but it can be found in some old bottles. Without going into details of how to calculate, see the correspondences for the most frequent grades in whiskey:

70° proof=40% of alcohol; 75° proof=42,85% of alcohol; 80° proof=45,7% of alcohol; 90° proof=51,4% of alcohol; 100° proof=57,1% of alcohol.

To complicate things further, the Americans still use another measurement system, which has nothing to do with the British. But the conversion to the Gay-Lussac system is much easier, the American proof grade represents exactly double the degree we know. That is, a whiskey with 101° proof corresponds to an alcohol of 50.5°.

The continuous distillation. Use the same fermented must, made from various cereals (especially corn) with the addition of malted barley. The still used is totally different. It is composed of two large copper columns that can reach a height of fifteen meters. The cold must reaches the first column, called rectifier, where it is heated by boiling water vapor. Next it is sent to the second column, the analyzer, where it passes by gravity through a succession of perforated rafts; when it passes, it finds a flow of water vapor that separates the lighter, drier elements. They return again to the first column, where they condense with the contact of the cold must that circulates permanently. The less volatile elements are reinjected into the circuit, while only the purest alcohols are progressively recovered and condensed.

All the grace of the system lies in continuous operation, thanks to this double change of heat: the cold must condense alcohol, which reheats it to be distilled. The production costs are lower, and the yield is higher: a continuous still on average can produce up to 40 million liters of alcohol per year, against 2.5 million a still. But the brandy produced is less aromatic.

Used in Scotland to obtain the grain whiskeys used to make the blends, the continuous still is the only one used in North America for the distillation of bourbons, whiskeys and Canadian whiskeys.

THE AGING

Whatever the chosen distillation method is, the obtained liquor is not yet whiskey. It lacks an aging time in wooden barrels, oak in most cases. Here, the time factor is decisive. There are a few legal minimums (three years in Scotland) to obtain the designation of origin, but aging is often much higher when you want to obtain high quality whiskeys.

In a barrel, complex changes are made between alcohol, ambient air and wood tannins. Also, the context plays an important role: the nature of the wood, its previous use, the temperature and the degree of humidity, the environmental aromas (like the marine iodized air that bathes the malts elaborated in Islay). New components appear, others merge to give rise to new aromas. But nothing can replace the time factor. It takes a minimum of eight to ten years for a malt to begin to reveal all its qualities, the maximum duration of aging is twenty to twenty-five years in the best cases. There are some exceptions, but it is not common, and whiskey reaches its maximum quality at the end of such period, while wine spirits may age for longer. The nature of the barrel greatly influences the final result, depending on whether it is new or if it has already served to preserve other spirits. For economic reasons, the Scots have reused the casks of Spanish sherry, discovering in this way the qualities that contributed to their malts. Later they took advantage of the American legislation, which prohibited the producers of bourbons and whiskeys from using old barrels; so they bought the American used barrels from distilleries. All combinations between barrels of different origins are possible, and are used by distillers to create their own style.

THE BLEND

As for cava, mixing, or blending, is an essential component for developing whiskey. Without this process, it is likely that scotch would have remained as a regional product, and would not have achieved the international notoriety it has.

It consists of mixing many dozens of whiskeys from different origins and ages in order to create a specific, easily identifiable style that resists the ups and downs of production. It all lies in the smell of the blender (since it is not a matter of drinking the different samples of whiskeys to decide whether or not they will be in the final recipe), capable of identifying the characteristics of the available whiskeys and of bringing them together to create and maintain a whiskey identical.

Each blend recipe is jealously protected, without remaining immovable. The real talent of the blender lies not in the ability to reproduce a recipe, but in being able to make the same whiskey from variable ingredients. Since, depending on the circumstances, some ingredients may be missing for a longer or shorter period. It is also possible to collect «single malts», which gives rise to the *vatted malts*, also called «pure malts». But this practice is less and less used, with the development of the commercialization of single malt.

Once the mixture is made in the tanks, in large capacity barrels, it is common for the whiskey to have a new aging time in other barrels, in order to completely harmonize the different constituents. Then comes the time of packaging, labeling and shipping. The whiskey is then ready for consumption and will no longer change. It may degrade eventually, if the bottle remains in contact with the oxygen in the air for a long time, once the bottle is opened.

THE PLEASURE OF TASTING

The choice of a whiskey depends on the moment it will be consumed. Is an incentive needed after a day's work? Do you need a «whiplash» after spending the day outdoors? Is it meant to create the environment in a meeting between friends? Is it to finish a good meal, accompanied by majestic cigars? In each of these cases, and in many others, the same whiskey will be more or less appropriate. There is no whiskey «for everything», capable of being appreciated in no matter what time or in what circumstance.

There are still some principles to be observed, in order not to diminish the talent of the distiller and the patience of the aging that has been put to obtain it.

Generally, the whiskeys available in bottles are 40°, sometimes 43°, even 46° in the case of American bourbons. There are also some «dry barrel», which can exceed 60°.

These are generally too high to be able to appreciate them as they deserve. Alcohol stuns the taste buds and nose receptors. It is necessary to dilute it a little. For this reason whiskey is consumed in Scotland and Ireland, served with a little fresh water (10° C maximum) and not gaseous. Each one adds the quantity he likes, to arrive at a diluted solution comprising between 20 and 30% of alcohol. This method, in addition to having the advantage of attenuating the strength of alcohol, also has the interest of awakening the aromas of whiskey, especially for smell. The other modes of consumption have more drawbacks. The gaseous water, especially, releases the carbonic gas that makes the appreciation of whiskey aromas more complex. As for ice cubes, they have the disadvantage of excessively cooling the whiskey, sometimes «frosting» its main aromatic characteristics. A simple example will suffice to prove it: fill two identical glasses with the same dose of the same whiskey. Add ice cubes in one, and in the other fresh water. The difference is impressive, to the point of making believe that it is two different liquors.

Throughout the world, the bar is a privileged place to discover new whiskeys.

USEFUL ADDRESSES
Warehouses and warehouses

In Scotland:
Cadenhead's, 172 Canongate, Edimburgo.
Gordon & Mac Phail, 58-60 South Street, Elgin.
Scotch Whisky Heritage Centre, 354 Castlehill, Edimburgo.

In London:
Oddbin's, 3 1-33 Weir Road, Wimbledon.
Harrod's, Knightsbridge.
Fortnum & Masón, 181 Piccadilly.
Milroy's, 3 Greek Street.
The Vintage House, 42 Oíd Compston Street.

ACKNOWLEDGMENTS
Murray Bremner, of United Distillers in London; MM. Benitah of the Maison du whiskey in Paris; Marc Sibard, from Caves Auge in Paris; Duncan Mac Elhone, from Harry's Bar in Paris; Timothy Goddard of Saint-James in Paris.

BIBLIOGRAFÍA
Michael Jackson, *Malt Whisky Companion*, Dorling Kindersley, London, 1994.
Michael Jacksón, *The World Guide to Whisky*, Dorling Kindersley, London, 1987.
Charles Mac Lean, *The Pocket Whisky Book*, Mitchell Bazley, Reed International, London, 1993.
James Darwen, *La Grande Histoire du whisky*, Flammarion, Paris, 1992.
James Darwen, *Whisky: le guide*, Hermé, París, 1995.